SOMETHING NEW IS HAPPENING

The Life and Times Of Naftali Bennett

MOSHE PITCHON

https://www.21stcenturyjudaism.com/

To Keren Or and Sivan
My two beautiful daughters
Inside and out
My life is blessed because of you

FOREWORD	5
CHAPTER 1	11
The High- tech Entrepreneur	11
CHAPTER 2	25
Netanyahu's Chief of Staff	25
Second Lebanon War	25
CHAPTER 3	37
The Wars that Changed Israel	37
CHAPTER 4	56
Habayt HaYehudi	56
CHAPTER 5	77
Bennett's Liberal Nationalism	77
CHAPTER 6	95
The New Right	95
CHAPTER 7	102
Education	102

CHAPTER 8 — 112
The Comeback Kid — 112

EPILOGUE — 124

REFERENCES — 128

Foreword

History used to be written years after events had happened. It took a long time to gather information and acquire the perspective necessary to understand what had happened.

This was most palpable in Jewish history when, as professor Salo W. Baron wrote, "[...] during the dispersion until about a hundred years ago, the Jewish people seem[ed] to have lost interest in writing even its own history."[1]

In other words, people were little, if at all, conscious that they were living in history and that historical changes were affecting them.

Naftali Bennett's surprising political coup (after all, even Benjamin Netanyahu seems to have been caught off-guard) occurred on June 31, 2021.

Bennett performed one of the most improbable political moves in Israel's political history, something that didn't happen accidentally. It had been at least 15 years in the making.

During that period of time, Bennett had been Netanyahu's chief of staff, head of three political parties, Minister of Economy, Education, Religious Services, Jerusalem and Diaspora Affairs, and Minister of Defense, unofficial Covid Zar, CEO of the Yesha Council and "Our Israel." And of course, now, Prime Minister.

All this is in pursuit of a vision that is so contemporary as to pardon if one feels that it belongs to the future. Bennett himself said it so when in 2016 he coined the political slogan that has been identifying him all along his relatively short political career:

"Something new is happening."

Because I live in one of the greatest democracies in the world, and I have also lived under military dictatorships, I probably appreciate how incredible a democracy Israel is, even when others consider it not to be so.

My appreciation stems primarily from the fact that I am a Jew.
Rabbi Irving Greenberg noted that for Jews, Israel "is *the* place where Jewish religion and Jewish morality are put to the test because there a Jewish majority decides policy." [2]

The determination of Israeli democracy is not, or should not be, based on comparing it with other experiences, other realities, other societies, other cultures but on what, the Jewish people, want and are willing to stand for. And, consequently, what their appointed leaders do in their name.

The political upheaval of the recent four elections in two years was based on a general awareness among Israelis (and maybe the rest of the world) that Benjamin Netanyahu- one of the most outstanding leaders the State of Israel had ever had- had overstayed his mandate.

One of the most challenging, and at the same time, frustrating conundrums facing Judaism, and in particular Israel, is the debilitating disagreements between how the past is understood and the future envisioned. Between the old and the new.

This confrontation is best expressed in the utterance of two rabbis whose influence in Jewish culture is incommensurable.

Rabbi Moses Schreiber, the "Hatam Sofer,"[3] synthetized the Jewish religious opposition to modernity expressed by the *Haredim*.[4]

"Judaism and the Jewish people would be safe, the Hatam Sofer believed, only to the extent that they regrouped around the traditional practices and were willing to live in accordance with a mythic past that was disconnected from the contemporary reality."[5]

Never say 'times have changed.' We have an old Father- praised be his name- who has never changed and never will change."[6]

The Hatam Sofer thus coined up the slogan that "the Torah forbids anything new in every place."[7]

Opposite to him is Rabbi Abraham Isaac Kuk,[8] "prophet of the liberal wing of Orthodoxy, which identified itself wholeheartedly with the Zionist enterprise, recognizing as their brothers in spirit and destiny the zealous nationalists who denied the sanctity of the Torah."[9]

"Kuk declared that the ancient must be modernized and the modern sacralized.

His proposed revolution by way of the profane was not an escape from religion but a way to revive it." [10]

Bennett belongs to the Jewish stream that has grown around the inspiration of Rabbi Kuk. He combines his personal energetic will and endurance with the mental tools developed by Rabbi Kuk, to stop the forces of obscurantism. These are the forces which are surreptitiously threatening to engulf and burn down this miracle which is the modern State of Israel.

I know I should avoid hyperbole in my appraisals and tone down my enthusiasm, if not my love. But, my experience is the number of times I have heard political leaders, social organizers, educators, industrialists, scientists, and countless others who have asked and ask:

"why can't we be like Israel and achieve what they have achieved in such a short amount of time?"

One answer may be, you may need a professional soldier that at a certain point decides that he has warred enough to protect his home and his family, and the time has come to apply many of those same skills to business.

And when he has made his first couple of millions in a short four years decides that it is enough and that now he has accumulated skills and experiences to revamp a moribund political party. When that is done successfully, he realizes that it is time for him to manage his country. He understands that like everything he has previously done; it has to be done competently, a task that is not made easier when his language- Hebrew-lacks a word for it.[11]

My objective has not been to write a biography or a political analysis. If anything, I have tried to put together different articles in the media into a coherent narrative.

My fundamental objective is to call attention to what is happening, the meaning of what people like Naftali Bennet are doing not only for Israel but, for Judaism, the Jews, and to benefit the world.

The model of the future Jew is the new generation of Israelis like Bennett, not those rooted in the old world.

As Shmuel Rosner and Camil Fuchs have written:

> "An Israeli Judaism is developing in Israel, with its own unique characteristics.[12]
>
> "The buds of a new Jewish culture in Israel are already visible. We shall call it "Israeli Judaism." This was practically inevitable, of course. Israel was founded to bring forth a new Judaism—to produce a culture that would allow Jews to live meaningful Jewish lives in the modern age."[13]

I wouldn't have been able to write about all this if it hadn't been because of the information and the analysis provided by Amotz Asa-El, Moti Caspit, Mazal Mualem, Haviv Reettig Gur, Anshel Pfeffer, Amos Harel, and many other incredibly qualified and professional Israeli journalists helping Israel to remain democratic.

There was a time when Jewish history, the political maneuvers, and competitions between kings, high priests, prophets, and rabbis were written based just on small inscriptions found on ostraca or incomplete phrases found in torn parchments discovered in caves or *genizot*.

Because of that, it may be that it took us so long, and we understood so partially what happened.

Today we are blessed with the abundance of the likes of *Haaretz, The Jerusalem Post, The Times of Israel, Al-Monitor, The New York Times, The Washington Post, Time magazine, The New Yorker, The Atlantic, Vanity Fair, Commentary, Moment Magazine,* and many others that write in-depth about Israel allowing us to compare narratives and fill gaps in the stories.

Not to speak of the marvel that are electronic books, that allow us to literally find at the tip of our fingers whole chunks of reasoned histories barely a few months old.

Without them, we would hardly know much about Israel, barely understand it, and miss a lot about ourselves.

Chapter 1

The High- tech Entrepreneur

The condemnations were vicious and unhindered. The *Haredi* rabbis were hysterically alarmed that the new government was going to "uproot all sign of Judaism from the land" and "trample over every value of the Torah."

The first Israeli prime minister who identified himself openly as religious was for the members of these religious blocs, "un-Jewish." "A brazen sinner, an evil man, who should remove his kippah."

The head of this parliamentary bloc of *Haredim* urged the religious-Zionist community from which most of the newly elected prime minister voters originated, to "vomit those people out, let them be excommunicated and banished from among you, remove them from the people of Israel…. We will make heaven and earthquake" against the new government, he vowed."[14]

Exertions to delegitimize weren't instigated solely by the regressive religious camp. Those belonging to the same political right-wing factions as the brand-new prime minister didn't shy a bit from calling him a "liar" and a "crook" either. A doctored photo of Naftali Bennett in an Arab *kaffiyeh*, with the words "The Liar" written above, had been promiscuously circulated.

Adding to the bloated ideological rhetoric, the now-ousted longest-serving prime minister in the history of the modern State of Israel- charged the man replacing him with betraying the political right because of political ambition.

Being part of a proportional political system of representation that enables almost every sector of the country's opinion to be represented in the *Knesset* [15] is a contact sport where showing civility is more times than not interpreted as a sign of weakness. Yet, this time there seemed to be something more. It was sheer panic, the anguish of sects and tribes dreading their becoming irrelevant. To hide the root of their vehemence, the parties being pushed out screamed: "Betrayal!"

Bennett didn't try to hide that before the election, he had said that a candidate with ten mandates could not be prime minister.
More than that, to make even more clear what he meant, he had added: "that is not Democracy."

The new right-wing head of Israel's 36th government had also vowed that he would not, under any circumstances, form a government with avowed centrist Yair Lapid or with ultra-left-wing and anti-Zionist parties.

That was then. Now he was doing all of the above.

For the previous two years, Benjamin Netanyahu had mostly been a caretaker Prime Minister. Four inconclusive elections in two years took care of this.
Each one of them sucking the little oxygen left into Israel's governance. With no party able to form a

majority coalition in the *Knesset*, the country was perilously shipwrecked.

Governments without mandates can't pass budgets, so a larger-than-anticipated budget deficit went unaddressed.

A new multi-year plan for the military languished. A much-needed infusion of funds for the health care system failed to materialize.

In addition, key state officials, including the state attorney and senior executive officers at the Justice and Finance ministries, went unappointed. In its 73-year history, the country had never found itself in such a situation.

Bennett, however, hadn't only made ideologically driven pledges. He had also made two additional practical commitments that demanded immediate attention if the substantial issues of the country were to be addressed.

The first was to prevent the fifth round of elections. The second: to replace Benjamin Netanyahu.

In confiding lawmakers in his party that he intended to form a government with the "change bloc" of anti-Netanyahu parties-an unprecedented coalition of parties spanning the whole range from left to right, in addition to an Islamist Arab party -he told them:

"You have to understand. We are not choosing between the two alternatives of a right-wing government or a 'change government.' We've turned over every stone. Netanyahu doesn't have the votes for a right-wing

government. How often do we have to batter the state with elections to understand there is no right-wing government? Leadership means taking responsibility. We have red lines, and we'll uphold them. We won't relinquish territory, and we won't harm the Jewish identity of the State of Israel. It's easy to hunker down and fan the flames of internal division as others do. But that's how you tear the nation apart. This is a national unity government of equal forces, and I don't apologize; I'm proud of our actions in the difficult circumstances. That's our essence — taking responsibility."

On a TV interview, he stressed once again the motivation behind his actions:

> *"The core promise in these elections was to get Israel out of the chaos…It's the easiest thing to entrench yourself in every promise. If everyone did that, no government would have been formed, and it happened after four elections. I knew I was going to be criticized, and in the choice between what's good for Israel and this thing, I chose what's good for Israel."*

He also knew what to expect:

> *"I told my kids that their father was going to be the most hated person in the country."*

Bennett was not alone in his assessment that Netanyahu, the longest-serving prime minister in Israel's history, had to step down. Seven other political parties besides his, and half the country, firmly believed that Netanyahu had overstayed his tenure as prime minister.

That, however, didn't insulate Bennett from the perception of a large chunk of the Israeli voters that he was an "opportunist."

This perception was reflected in the unprecedented low electoral margin gotten by Bennet.

No prime minister in Israel had ever entered office with less than a quarter of the 120 seats in parliament, Bennett's party, *Yamina*, had garnered only six seats.
The leader of a minor right-wing party that only a few months earlier had failed to cross the necessary electoral vote to qualify for its place in the Knesset had successfully maneuvered to become head of the Israeli government.

A month after his appointment, a poll conducted by market research company Midgam showed that 40% of Israelis still would have chosen Netanyahu as their prime minister, 24% would have selected Yair Lapid, and only 14 % would have selected Bennett.

Bennett's opportunity to ascend to a position of maximum influence in the country's direction came when after the fourth inconclusive election in two years, neither the pro-Netanyahu bloc parties nor the anti-Netanyahu group could form a majority without his tiny party.

Such is the nature of the Israeli proportional system of representation.

Pro and anti-Netanyahu bloc parties had courted him. Both had offered him a chance to serve as prime minister in a rotation agreement. Though the *Likud*, Netanyahu's party, had won 30 seats in the election, more than any other party, he was still short of the minimum 61 seats required to form a government.

With the endorsement of the ultra-Orthodox parties and a far-right alliance, Netanyahu's coalition would have still only gathered 52 seats. With Bennett joining in, the Netanyahu coalition would have been closer to form a government but still not there.

> *"I have just heard Netanyahu's proposal… I asked for a government. And that, to my regret, he does not have one."* Bennett said at the time.

On the other hand, with Bennett's backing and seven more of the 13 parties that won seats in the March 23, 2021 election, centrist leader Yair Lapid succeeded in putting together a coalition that met the required 61 votes.

Thirty-five minutes before the midnight deadline, President Reuven Rivlin's phone rang.

> "I am honored to inform you that I have succeeded in forming a government," Lapid told Rivlin. "The government will be an alternate government following Clause 13(a) of the Basic

Law: The Government and Member of the Knesset Naftali Bennett will serve as a prime minister first."

"Opportunism" is questionable behavior, particularly in politics. It hangs on the delicate balance between statesmanship and selfishness.

It is in the nature of politics that sometimes it is necessary to stick to principles while at other times the interest of immediate needs demand deferral.

For Bennett to move from a right to a center-left coalition had not been easy.

He grew up in a very right-wing political home and was active in rightist youth groups. However, he, and all the other members of his coalition, had mastered the art of compromise.

The newly elected prime minister and all the government members he headed understood very well that inflexible, non-negotiable political principles are not politics but sectarianism.

For sure, Bennett wasn't all of one- mind with some of Lapid's tenets. Yet, he was also very much aware that behind the ideological divide, they both shared a similar scale of values. What mattered now was breaking the electoral impasse that had dragged down the country for the last two years.

On his address to the *Knesset* ahead of the confidence vote that would seat him as the head of the Israeli government, Bennet said:

> *"This is a special moment. The moment the baton of leading the people and the country passes – as in a relay race – to the next generation. Each generation has its challenges, and out of each generation comes the leaders that can overcome them."*

The June 31, 2021 vote of confidence that appointed Israel's 36th government is a significant watershed in Israel politics. It represents the particular way of thinking of a new kind of Israelis, those fully immersed in the 21st century.

After the state's founders and Netanyahu's generation, Naftali Bennett belongs to the third generation of Israeli leaders.

He is the first kipa-wearing, Sabbath-observing religious Jew to run the country; the first to have lived in a settlement; the first to share power with an Arab party.

A commando-turned-millionaire high-tech entrepreneur who isn't interested in making another million but who wishes to bring to the management of his country the kind of vision and commitment that defines his generation.

Born in 1972-one year before the passing away of Israel's first prime minister David Ben-Gurion-Bennett, like uncountable other young Israelis, was raised in a society focused on solving problems and adapting to change as quickly as possible. Young Israelis doing their military service are pressed to stretch themselves to the extreme limit of their abilities, forcing themselves to be brave and do complex and unpleasant things.

Strongly influenced by the army's practices and the world of high tech- business, young Israelis are encouraged to question conventional wisdom insistently, not for the sake of it but to ensure that what they believe renders their lives more meaningful and, thus, more worthwhile. They are also trained to be constantly on the look for opportunities.

This attitude has placed the State of Israel among the world's leading countries, contributing to humankind's welfare through medical cures, technological advancements, agricultural innovation, and humanitarian aid.

This is the mindset that motivated Bennett while studying law and business administration at the Hebrew University of Jerusalem in 1996 to begin working in the high-tech industry. First in software, then in quality assurance, and later in sales.

The late 1990s was a period of massive growth in the use and adoption of the Internet. Between 1999 and 2014 alone, Israeli entrepreneurs had started 10,185 high-tech companies, 2.6% of them with $100 million in annual revenues. "Every reasonable idea with good people got funding," said Bennett. So, in 1999, at the age of 27 and in his fourth year at the Hebrew University Bennett, he decided to seize the opportunity.

He met with Ben Enosh, a friend from his army time who introduced him to Michal Tsur, with whom he studied at the Hebrew University Secondary School ("Leyada"). Michal, in turn, brought her roommate Lior Golan. The four met at a park in Jerusalem and decided to create a start-up. They weren't sure what they would be developing, but they started working at the attic of one of the partners' fathers' homes, which had Internet and telephone access.

After three weeks and, after going through "some crazy ideas" (including special helmets to wear inside of cars), the idea of an online computer security product came up, a virtual credit card that would enable one-time purchases.

> *"We quickly built a very basic business plan," recalled Bennet, "and met with one of the less senior executives at Israel Seed Partners. He liked our idea and brought us to meet the rest of the partners. At one point in the meeting with them, we were asked how much money we wanted, and without batting an eyelid, we told him we needed $2 million."*

The company they formed was called Cyota. From the four partners, only Lior Golan had any technical training. Now Dr. Michal Tsur, who in 2006 would cofound an open-source video platform with $166 million in funding from Goldman Sachs and Sap, among others, said that Bennett

> "was the most charismatic, spoke better than the rest of us, and could present things better than anyone. And he was a quick study when it came to picking up the skills to be a very good manager. He is adept at tactical management and knows how to manage people. "The thing that characterizes Naftali best is that he learns from his mistakes. When he is criticized or gets feedback, he internalizes it and then modifies his behavior."[16]

Bennett and his wife had been living at the time in the West Bank settlement of Beit Aryeh for just a few months. Then the CEO job of Cyota demanded that they move to a major financial center where they could rouse interest in the newly formed company. In 2000 they moved to Manhattan.

> *"We raised, in stages, $12 million for development of the first product," Bennett said. "But it turned out we had an Indian and an Irish competitor, and they kicked our ass. Then the tech bubble burst. We had, like, three years in the company of shit," he recalled. "It was just survival. I went all over the country with my laptop." Gilat, his wife, meanwhile, was working as a pastry chef in chic Manhattan restaurants.*

> *"We were living in a student apartment, scrounging to make ends meet to save the company. I lived in New York for four years, during which I did not know if I was going to make it to the end of the month,"* he said.
>
> *"We scraped through for two years,"* he kept on going, *"and that whole time continued to come up with new initiatives. Most failed. We ran out of money. In the end, there was a slight chance for survival. Some investors said that if we were able to raise a million dollars, they would bring in $2.5 million. We managed to raise $800,000, and then one of the partners raised the remaining $200,000 from his grandmother. From that point on, we no longer worried about the company; we no longer worried about the product. We only wanted to repay his grandmother."* [17]

They had a hard time finding a bank willing to bankroll the single-use credit card for Internet purchases they had created. So, they started looking for whatever other unsatisfied needs in the world of credit cards, Internet purchases, security, and fraud they could find. "At some point," Dr. Tsur explains, "phishing became an issue - people getting emails that were ostensibly from their bank, but it wasn't their bank sending the emails-. We came along and developed a solution."

"Golan, Cyota's former chief technology officer, recalls persuading Bennett to make the change that put the company on the road to success and big money:

"We managed to bring the company to a place where we already had significant sales, but then we got stuck again. We came out with a product we believed would achieve growth for us, but it didn't do well. Naftali was sitting in New York, I was in Israel, and then I had the idea for a different spin on the product, which, given the market's dynamic, could have led to the breakthrough we were hoping for. We tried to nudge him via instant messaging for a month or two, but he didn't have the time to listen.
"Finally, I flew to New York and asked him to go shopping with me ... He suddenly had time, and I told him about my idea - and his jaw just dropped. That is what led to the breakthrough, the idea that transformed Cyota. He is very focused on attaining his goal and sometimes doesn't listen to what is happening around him. But when he does hear you, he is open to altering his way of thinking." [18]

"Their eventual success," wrote Haaretz journalist Anshel Pfeffer, " owed nearly as much to Bennett's perseverance and confident charm as the main salesman – and their product was a big success in helping banks curb online fraud. It was that confidence that got Cyota sold for $145 million to RSA Security in 2005 before it ever turned a profit.

"Naftali did a very good job handling the potential buyers," Tsur recalls. "Essentially, there was another buyer who placed a bid on the table a few weeks before the sale. It was much lower, but what was important to us was protecting the employees and keeping Cyota in Israel. In retrospect, we made a mistake selling, because we sold too cheap. At the time, we had something like $10 million in sales, and now it's nearly $200 million.

But we had to decide if we would continue taking risks and growing the company, and we decided it was time to sell. Naftali led the negotiations, and we pulled off a world-class maneuver. RSA was certain their direct competitor was about to buy us, so they put in a higher bid."[19]

After splitting the proceeds of the sale of Cyota, in 2005, with three partners and various rounds of investors, he came away with three or four million dollars before taxes. More than enough not to work for a long while and to make some investments, he said, "but not enough, so the kids don't have to work."[20]

Following the exit, Bennett remained with Cyota for six more months. Then, like thousands of other Israelis, he received an emergency call-up order to serve in the Second Lebanon War.

Chapter 2

Netanyahu's Chief of Staff

Second Lebanon War

> *"I had just sold a company for $145 million. I was supposed to be partying, flying off to the Caribbean, and instead, I found myself fighting in south Lebanon against terrorists who want to destroy my state."*

On July 12, 2006, at 9. 05 a.m. Hezbollah terrorists hidden on the Israeli side of the border fence that separates it from Lebanon hit two IDF[21] armored vehicles with at least one roadside bomb and rocket-propelled grenades. Simultaneously other Hezbollah teams were staging diversionary bombardments with mortars and Katyusha rockets on nearby IDF outposts and the northern Israeli settlements of Zarit and Shetula.

Thirty minutes after the attack on the armored vehicles, the IDF found that three of its soldiers were killed in the assault and that three others were wounded. Two additional Israeli soldiers, Sgt. First Class Ehud Goldwasser and Staff Sgt. Eldad Regev had been abducted.

A Merkava tank and an IDF platoon in armored personnel carriers crossed the border in pursuit of the captors. At around 11 a.m., four crew members were killed when the tank struck an improvised 200–300 kg explosive device (IED) planted by the terrorist group. An eighth soldier was killed in heavy fighting with a local Hezbollah cell.

While the military high command ordered armored columns to assemble and begin shelling Hezbollah rocked positions in Southern Lebanon and, the air force attacked suspected launching sites as far north as Beirut, Ehud Olmert, the Israeli prime minister, declared the abduction "an act of war," and made the Lebanese government responsible.

The head of the Israeli government warned his counterpart in Beirut that "the sky will fall on Lebanon" if the terrorists were not reined in and the abducted soldiers were not repatriated. "Our response will be very restrained," he promised. "But very, very, very painful."

Eventually, the entire air force and six IDF divisions, and the navy were involved in what would be thirty-four days of fighting.

Drafted into the IDF at 18, Bennet had chosen to go into an officer-training course. He earned his way into the grueling *Sayeret Matkal*.[22] This being the same elite commando that trained two other Israeli prime ministers: Benjamin Netanyahu and Ehud Bark.

After earning an officer commission, he took over command of a mysterious high-tech unit operating deep behind enemy lines. the *Maglan* commando unit. Now, at the age of 34, as dozens of *Maglan* soldiers were being airlifted into South Lebanon by helicopter, Bennett, whose expertise was in hunting down rocket launchers behind enemy lines, joined in again in what he considered literally defending "my family." The northern city of Haifa where his parents lived was being directly threatened by Lebanese missile fire, *"taking down a rocket in Lebanon was very personal for my family."* [23]

As the confrontation progressed, Hezbollah kept a steady barrage of rockets into northern Israel. The airlifted Maglan soldiers behind enemy lines in Lebanon kept calling in airstrikes against Hezbollah rocket launchers and headquarters, trucks, ammunition dumps, and other military infrastructure. Though Maglan's action reduced rocket fire on Israel's northern towns by about 40%, Bennet was deeply frustrated:

> *"Every day at 2 or 3 P.M., I would call through the radio my commanders to suggest this or that, and they would say, 'No, no, wait until evening, we'll talk then.' But you don't win wars by doing nothing."*

Echoing the feeling of many Israelis at the time, Bennett said: *"We failed-the Army—"failed. It was a draw at best."* Israel had done too little to take the war to Hezbollah in southern Lebanon. The command structure was confused and timid; the politicians lacked in resolve. *"There was a profound problem of spirit in the desire to win,"* he said.[24]

Devastated when a best friend was killed in the fighting, he decided not to return to the business world after the war.

> *"What I saw in that war is friends of mine injured or dying because of incompetent or immoral leadership." "It drove me almost crazy — how much good people are suffering because of bad leaders. That's what drove me into politics."* [25]

In December 2005, Benjamin Netanyahu had succeeded Ariel Sharon as leader of the Likud party. Bilha Nesson, a party activist, had introduced him to Ayelet Shaked, a young computer engineer, to manage his office. A one-term former prime minister,[26] Netanyahu was facing a daunting task trying to make what many considered an improbable comeback to head the government.

At the end of March 2006, Israelis had voted for the seventeenth Knesset, giving Netanyahu a decisive defeat.[27] Shaked, whose father typically voted for Likud and, who had acquired her defining political inspiration from reading Ayn Rand's "The Fountainhead" and "Atlas Shrugged," felt that the former prime minister was "in a political desert."

"The problem in the Likud," she said at the time, "is that every leader takes the Likud to the left."[28]

Though they had agreed that she would start working in May, her obligations with her current employer at the time, Texas Instruments, forced her to postpone taking over her new job with Netanyahu until September. The War in Lebanon was over by then, and, on August 21, protests calling for the government's resignation had begun.

Four days later, over 2,000 people participated in a march. The criticism of how Ehud Olmert and his government had handled the War presented Netanyahu with a new opportunity to replace him.

"The Netanyahu Shaked encountered in September," wrote Ben Caspit, "was completely different from the beaten man she'd agreed to work for in May. "I'm going to be prime minister," he informed her when she arrived for work."[29]

She was tasked almost at once with finding the right campaign manager. Lacking the necessary political experience, she asked her Tel Aviv University friend Erez Eshel to help her find a campaign director for Netanyahu.

Eshel, a West Bank settler who had served with Bennett in Sayeret Maglan, arranged for Shaked to meet Bennett at a café near his home in Ra'anana, a leafy, middle-class city outside Tel-Aviv.

Ganit Buganim, a classmate of Bennett's and Bnei Akiva member-the youth group where Bennett was a counselor in Haifa-recalls young Naftali, attending all the group's activities "with Yoni Netanyahu's book and read to the members of his group from it."[30]

Yonatan Netanyahu- Binyamin's elder brother had been killed in 1976 while leading a rescue mission at Entebbe, Uganda. He had been Naftali's hero his whole youth. Bennett admired the Netanyahus. He named his first son Yoni.

Bennett doesn't seem to have created much of an impression on Shaked at the meeting. However, she reported to Netanyahu that she thought she might have found a candidate for the chief of staff with his same mindset.

Netanyahu had some people check him further. "Instead of persuading me that he was suitable for Bibi, he kept asking whether Bibi was worthy of having him work for him," a Netanyahu confidant who met Bennett said at that time."[31] A couple of years later at a conference, Bennett would say in front of Netanyahu himself that he had joined him in 2006 *"to help the nationalist camp return to the country's leadership."* That was why he left the high-tech world.

"The chemistry between them anyhow was instant," writes Ben Caspit. Bennett was just what Netanyahu liked, a freshly minted tech millionaire whose mother tongue was English. He wore a tiny yarmulke on his head; espoused Religious Zionism; and was talented, articulate, right-wing, and a staunch admirer of Bibi. They clicked instantly. Netanyahu understood that Bennett would march him into the Facebook era, into tech, and toward Generation Y. Ostensibly, this was a marriage made in heaven." [32]

In late 2006 the then 33-year-old tech millionaire, former elite commando, had become in charge of preparing Netanyahu for the 2009 general election. This election would put him in office for the second time. Netanyahu seemed to had put together an office dream team that was supposed to accompany him to the Prime Minister's Office. [33]

The Likud party was actively involved in supporting the anti-Olmert protests pressing for the government's accountability. Tech tycoon Eli Ayalon who would later be appointed Likud's campaign manager personally by Netanyahu, was one of the organizers. So was Yoav Horowitz, who would later declare, "I helped Netanyahu in a professional role, not a political role, in the 2006 primary."[34] Horowitz had been called on a later campaign for the January 2013 general election: Netanyahu's "operations officer" for organizing demonstrations by army reservists after the 2006 Second Lebanon War. Two more of Bennett's close friends, Erez Eshel and Yakir Segev, played critical roles in the movement to topple Olmert.

Netanyahu's campaign had certainly every interest to keep the protests going as long as possible to erode Olmert's popular support. Netanyahu himself, however, kept a low profile. As a returnee from the war, Bennett not only made common cause with the reservists, he understood the protests to carry the political intention the Likud was aiming at, toppling Olmert.

The protests had succeeded in establishing an inquiry commission on the government's conduction of the war, making its interim conclusions public on April 30, 2007.

Bennett decided to push a reservists' anti-Olmert protest in May and add to it, bereaved families and other groups. He even recruited various left-wing organizations.

"After being nonpartisan throughout the Second Lebanon War," Barak Ravid commented, "Netanyahu suddenly found himself cast as someone who was trying to subvert the government and exploiting the reservists and bereaved families for political gain."[35]

If this didn't make Netanyahu look good, that the campaign hadn't succeeded in toppling Olmert didn't help him either.

Though Bennett had become part of the team behind Netanyahu's education reform and ran Netanyahu's campaign ahead of the primary elections for the leadership of Likud, the failed campaign to oust Olmert had thawed Netanyahu's appreciation of Bennett.

Things in the office, in the meantime, weren't going well either

As soon as Bennet had arrived, two camps in the office had formed. On one of them were Bennett and Shaked.

"Bennett and Shaked felt that precious time was being constantly wasted in unnecessary arguments with

Netanyahu's wife who didn't move from her husband's side and tangled herself in the office affairs.

They certainly did not like her involvement in setting Netanyahu's daily schedule or her demands that they cancel meetings or his participation in various events because of family or other considerations.

Then, Bennett committed the cardinal sin of saying to Sara, who demanded a full report on Bibi's whereabouts, "I work for your husband, not for you."[36]

On March 10, 2008, the Israeli *Yedioth Ahronot* published an investigative report. It revealed that Netanyahu had paid part of Bennett and Shaked's salary out of his own pocket after having difficulty finding sources of funding the many advisers around him. For all that time, Sarah Netanyahu did not know about the financial arrangement. She reacted angrily when she found out that her husband was paying his advisers from his personal bank account.

According to the published testimonies, Sarah Netanyahu harshly criticized Bennett and Shaked for the two-receiving payment from her husband's private pocket .She announced that the settlement was canceled and that they were required to return any money they had received in this way to the family. Bennett and Shaked then refused to comment on the publication of the investigation and never denied its findings.

On March 31, 2009, Netanyahu became the prime minister of Israel's 32nd government. Bennett did not accompany him. He had lasted at Netanyahu's office barely a year and a half

When he served as Netanyahu's chief of staff, Bennett had stayed in touch with Lior Golan, one of his partners at *Cyota*. They were both investing on their own in high-tech companies and young entrepreneurs when they learned about a young company called *Soluto*, which was developing solutions for the automatic diagnosis and correction of computer problems.

In November 2009, *Soluto* had embarked on a second round of raising investment funds. Golan and Bennett tried to help them get money from Bessemer, an Israeli venture capital fund. Bessemer knew and respected Bennett because they had invested in *Cyota*. They wanted him to be part of the company's management, and they put this as a condition for providing the funds.

> "Bennett," Roee Adler, chief product office of Soluto, said, "is an extraordinarily brilliant, talented, smart person. Until recently, I would consult with him on business matters daily. He helped us a great deal; he contributed to the company. As a business person, one of his strongest focuses was to do the minimum required to achieve a maximum result – and then move on to the next minimum. He is very efficient, very much the doer. There are greater idols than him in the high-tech field, but he's a real pistol."[37]

Yashi Green, who, together with Tomer Dvir, had co-founded *Soluto,* told *Haaretz* that they had received the funding thanks to Bennett.

In early February 2010, just after three months, Bennett announced he was leaving. He said that he had to fulfill his own ideals, that he was awfully concerned about the way Likud was being run, that he could no longer wait, and that he had to start influencing.

Adam Fisher, a partner at Bessemer, was not pleased. "He was part of the main reason we invested," Fisher says. "We tend to believe entrepreneurs with whom we've had past success. After three months, he upped and left.
We were surprised and angry. "Deep down," he adds, "we respect someone who says, 'I've done enough on the business side, and now I want to contribute,' even if you don't identify with the direction he's taking.
But if we had known he was casting about for a political option, we wouldn't have taken him on. We invested large sums of money, and it was unpleasant."[38]

Soluto cofounder Green, on the other hand, says he is not angry about the way Bennett left: "As soon as he saw we were getting along without him, he pulled the cord on his parachute. Thanks to him, we got the money."[39]

"Neil Cohen and Michael Eisenberg, former partners in the VC fund Israel Seed Ventures, invested in

Cyota and also contributed toward Bennett's campaign in the primary.

Cohen says he tried to dissuade Bennett from going into politics but is happy he did: "I met with him after Cyota was sold, asked him what was next, and he said, 'Something in the public realm.' I argued that he could contribute more if he built another Cyota. I tried to persuade him that he would best serve Israel by building another company and creating even more jobs, but he was determined.

"Seven years ago, I thought he should stay in high tech, but now the facts speak for themselves ... If I were asked today, I'd no longer advise him to build another high-tech company because he is capable of much more. Now I want him to bring his abilities to the political arena and hope all of the people of Israel will benefit."[40]

Five years after selling *Cyota* and serving as minister of Economy, Nashville-based *Asurion* acquired *Soluto* for a reported $100 million $130 million. As an investor and CEO of Soluto, Bennett earned what some sources said was a "significant" amount of money from the deal

Chapter 3

The Wars that Changed Israel

> "Very heavy machine and mortar fire, probably cannon, continuous in Jerusalem," reported the British consul-general at around 11: 30 a. m. "It looks as though Jordanians were pouting a lot into the New City. Jerusalem totally engulfed in war. Bullets have already hit the consulate, one narrowly missing Her Majesty's Consul."[41]

Intermittent machine-gun exchanges had been going across most of Jewish Jerusalem since 9: 30 a.m. on Monday, June 5, 1967. The Jordanian forces kept escalating the fighting gradually. The shelling lasted ten hours, killing twenty civilians and injuring over one thousand.

Three weeks earlier, on May 16, General Ibrahim Sharqawy, chief of the Egyptian General Staff, had sent a note to Major General Indar Jit Rikhye- the Indian commander of the United Nations Emergency Force (UNEF) in Sinai. The three 400-man international force had been in Egypt since 1957. Their task has been to deter warfare during periods of intense Arab-Israeli friction, keep infiltrators from exiting Gaza, and ensure free passage through the Straits of Tiran. The note sent by the Egyptian chief of Staff ordered the United Nations commander to virtually clear his entire force out of Egyptian territory.

The next day, radio Saut-Al- Arab" proclaimed: "The whole country of Egypt, with its entire human, economic and scientific potential, is ready to launch a total war against Israel."
Then, Egyptian planes coming from Jordan violated Israeli airspaces. Three days later, Israel Chief of Staff Yitzhak Rabin informed the Israeli cabinet that in an unprecedented build-up threatening peace, Egyptian troops massed on the border with Israel had increased from 35,000 to 80,000.

At 4 a.m. on May 23, Israel's prime minister Levi Eshkol had been awakened by a call from Israel's Chief of Staff, Yitzhak Rabin: news had just been received from Cairo that Egyptian President Gamal Abdel Nasser had announced the closure of the Straits of Tiran. In 1967, 90% of Israeli oil passed through this narrow sea passageway between the Sinai and Arabian peninsulas that the world community had recognized as an international waterway.

Closing the Straits meant a war declaration.

A majority of Western countries' embassies had advised their nationals to leave Israel. And as a bad omen sign, the first representatives of the International Red Cross had arrived and offered their services. Chief of staff Rabin instructed schools and other public buildings to be readied to serve as hospital and casualty centers. The chief rabbinate sent rabbis to sanctify public parks to serve as cemeteries. Pharmacists reported that some concentration camp survivors were begging for poisons so that if Israel was overcome, they would not fall once again into an enemy's hands."[42]

Hebrew University professor Yosef Ben-Shlomo recalled:

> "While waiting for the war, many *sabras* underwent a psychic upheaval- identification with Holocaust Jewry and determination that "It won't happen here." Suddenly the peril of annihilation was in the air, and a decision was taken: even if we are killed, we won't return to Auschwitz. May 1967 added a historical dimension to the *sabra*'s mindset, as well as an existential comprehension that we have no one but ourselves."[43]

The three weeks that preceded June 5 when the war broke out were an agonizing nerve-racking period. Suddenly the peril of annihilation had polluted the air breathed by Israeli and Jews around the world.

> "Three factors help explain the widespread fear among Israelis. First, the enduring national trauma of the Holocaust, which thousands of Israelis personally experienced, has always played a central role in the political, cultural, and psychological socialization of all Israeli Jews. The main lesson most Jews derive from the Holocaust was that it could happen again because such an event happened once. The second factor was the enormity of weaponry and forces amassed during the latter part of May

1967 all along three of Israel's borders. This coupled with pronouncements by Arab leaders about the Jewish state's imminent destruction (For example, Ahmad Shuqairi, the president of the Palestine Liberation Organization, declared: "There will be practically no Jewish survivors."). Third, there was a widespread sense of political isolation, which grew out of the failure of the United Nations and U. S. President Lyndon Johnson to soften Egypt's aggressive posture."[44]

Finally, at 7:10 a.m. on Monday, June 5, 1967, Waves of Israeli warplanes took off from the Israeli airfield at Hazor. Sweeping beneath the enemy radar, they struck Egypt's airbases. Before 8:00 a.m., the ground assault began in Sinai. At 4:00 p.m., an Egyptian officer would arrive at President Gamal Abdel Nasser's office with the information: "I have come to tell you that we no longer have an air force."

That same morning Jordan's King Hussein had heard from the Egyptian President different kind of news: Egypt was obliterating Israel's military.

In his memoirs, Chief of Staff Rabin recalls:

> "our instructions from the government were to refrain from acting on any other front other than the Egyptian front. Our planes were to be used only in response to overt provocation. Israel clearly did not want a war with Jordan."[45]

However, on the morning of June 5, the Arab Legion had already massed 255 tanks and 144 artillery pieces in the West Bank and East Jerusalem. Three additional infantry brigades were left in the East Bank, joined by two Egyptian commando battalions. Iraqi expeditionary force, consisting of four brigades, one of them armored and one mechanized, began moving into eastern Jordan that same day. The Saudis had also joined in sending elements of a brigade.

Earlier that morning in Jerusalem, General Odd Bull- the UN commander -had been summoned to the Israeli Foreign Ministry. A veteran UN specialist at the Ministry, Arthur Lourie, asked Bull to urgently convey to King Hussein that "Israel will not attack Jordan if Jordan maintains the quiet. But if Jordan opens hostilities, Israel will respond with all of its might."

The decision to warn Hussein had been made at the cabinet meeting a day earlier and was also delivered to Jordan via the U.S. embassy: "Israel had no aggressive intentions toward Jordan."

Later, King Hussein would admit to having received the warning:

> "[Israel warned that] if we did not intervene, they would save us from consequences which otherwise were inevitable: but by that time, we no longer had any choice. We were obliged to do everything to help our allies."

At 1:00 p. m., after having been shelling the suburbs of Tel Aviv, Ramat Aviv, and Jerusalem for the whole morning, the Arab legion crossed the Jerusalem armistice lines.

The Jordanian forces entered the neutral zone and surrounded the United Nations headquarters on the so-called Hill of Evil Counsel. This building had been the Government House during the thirty years that Britain had ruled the land, which had been defined according to the biblical boundaries of "Dan to Beersheba."

This "was an open invitation to the Israelis to move in," wrote Evan Wilson, the United States minister- consul in Jerusalem, who witnessed these events. "[46] Historian, and future Israeli ambassador to the United States Michael B. Oren, reflected: "Had the Jordanian refrained from seizing Government Hill, the region would have looked much different."[47]

Once the lines were crossed and the area occupied, the Israelis had no other choice but to launch in a wholly defensive war.

At 2:00 p. m. General Uzi Narkiss, commander of the central front, summoned Col. Motta Gur, the commander of the 55th Brigade in the battle for Jerusalem, to his headquarters: The paratroopers were being sent to Jerusalem.

Two days later, on June 7, ravaged by the aerial strafing and bombing, Jordan's Twenty-fifth infantry and Fortieth Armored brigades collapsed as fighting units.

What would become a six-day war had, in its inception, a very limited objective: to force Nasser to lift its waterways blockade by neutralizing the Egyptian air force and its first line of defense in the Sinai. That the war escalated was largely the result of Jordan's military intervention on behalf of Egypt.
Under pressure and mislead,[48] Jordan went into a war that the Israeli government had made every effort to prevent[49].

King Hussein had gambled half the kingdom his father, King Abdullah, acquired in 1948 through war. As a consequence of its self-defense needs, Israel had no choice other than to take those territories back.

The immediate Israeli government position was that the lands it now held were assets that would be bargained at peace negotiations. In fact, Israel was more interested in achieving peace and recognition from its neighbors than in enlarging its territory. Not soon after the war, Israeli prime minister Levi Eshkol offered to return the territories to the Arabs if they would recognize Israel and negotiate peace.

In an interview with the BBC on June 12, 1967, Defense Minister Moshe Dayan had famously said: "We are waiting for King Hussein to ring us...."

The call didn't come and, it became increasingly evident to Israel that the territories had been, in the words of Nobel Prize winner Eli Wiesel, "imposed" on them. Arab rejectionism became fully clear when eight Arab heads of state meeting at a summit in Khartoum in September 1967, enunciated their position with three emphatic 'nos':

> no recognition of Israel,
>
> no negotiations,
>
> no peace!

Arguably, then, the government of Israel had no intention of enlarging their territory before they engaged in a war of self-defense. The behavior during the May-June 1967 crisis demonstrates that its leaders wanted to avoid war. Not only was no war plan to occupy territory: once the war ended, the Israeli government spent several months looking to return those lands in exchange for peace.

"When Israelis think of the Six-Day War," says historian and former Israel's Ambassador to the U.S., Michael Oren, "they look at the capture of Jerusalem as the high point of the war, but in fact, it was unintentional."[50] This element of lack of human intentionality is probably the critical strengthening factor in the Jewish conception of knowledge that affirms that true meaning lies beyond what human eyes can see."

If from a military and political perspective, the aftermath of this war was an accident of history, the consequence of a series of Arab miscalculations, for those who believe that God is the Creator and guide of everything, this was certainly no accident. On the contrary, though human beings had intended only to free the closing of their waterways, God had another plan.

Indeed, for Jews, whose identity is framed by Biblical tenets as they are understood by Rabbinism, accepting the 1949 armistice borders had always been taken as a temporary political necessity, not a surrendering of their faith.

Mindful of the Talmudic dictum that "war is the beginning of Redemption,"[51] the Six-Day War brought the sense, particularly among certain religious Zionists such as the students of the *Mercaz ha- Rav* Yeshiva in Jerusalem, that current events were part of the drama of the End, and that they were the instruments of Divine redemption. However, it was not them the only ones moved by the encounter with the land of their historical identity.

> "When the paratroops arrived at the Western Wall, their deep feelings made them weep. These were not religiously observant troops, and the shofar blasts sounded by the IDF chief rabbi, Shlomo Goren, did not speak to them. But something in that encounter with Jewish history, with the Wailing Wall, shook them to the very roots of their being." Wrote historian Anita Shapira "the enthusiasm that engulfed the entire Jewish people, in Israel and the Diaspora, with the conquest of Jerusalem, highlighted hidden

desires and previously unsuspected levels of consciousness and identification."[52]

So, it was not surprising to find that after the Khartoum rebuff, 73 percent of the Israelis polled were not ready to return most of the forfeited territories. Now Religious Zionists, some of them looking forward to rebuilding the Temple in Jerusalem, impassioned nationalists, and security specialists all argued for a Greater Israel.

Arab refusal after Israel's conclusive military victory had energized an Israeli Right that had been almost dormant for decades. It was the religious Jews the ones that took the initiative. They produced a movement of settlers claiming an eternal right to all of the Jews' Biblical land. In the absence of treaties with its neighbors, they forced Israel's government to create "facts."

Six years later, at 2 p.m., on Saturday, October 6, 1973, Shabbat and Yom Kippur, the holiest day of the Jewish year, it happened all over again.

Six hundred- fifty-five Syrian artillery pieces and over 100 aircrafts were unleashed in a surprise attack in the north against Israel.

In the south, a rebuilt-and now one of the largest standing armies in the world- an Egyptian force consisting of 600,00 men, 2,000 thanks, 2,300 artillery pieces, 160 SAM missile batteries, and 550 combat planes launched against Israel.

Bar-Ilan University's Rector Harold Fisch recalls:

> "No one dared to doubt this time that we were under threat of annihilation. This was no normal international dispute, no quarrel about borders. It required no special gift for making historical analogies to see that in the joint onslaught on Israel made by the Arab armies and their helpers from a dozen lands, there was a genocidal intent, a continuation of Hitler's war against the Jewish people. The issue was not this or that piece of land; the issue was Israel's right to national existence, the Jewish people's right to physical space. But there was a metaphysical dimension also. The war was launched on Yom Kippur because it was thought that on that day, the front-line soldiers would be less on the alert than on other days of the year- this was an important tactical consideration." [53]

At a tremendous cost for Israel, the surprise attack launched by both Egypt and Syria was eventually fended off. Yet, a mood of depression and doubt settled on the country.

> "Atop the Hermon position, Colonel Avraham Ayalon, a veteran of the Givati Brigade in the 1948 war, found the body of his eldest son. In the dead of night, Major General Amos Horev dragged the body of his son-in-law from a trench near the line of the Egyptian Third Army. During a briefing session, General Chaim Bar-

> Lev was informed that his nephew had been killed in action. And on and on, some families losing more than one son, many suffering losses well beyond those of the 1967 war. It was a war of fathers and sons."[54]

The loss of more than 3,000 Israeli soldiers was proportionately the equivalent of 170,000 dead Americans, more than three times U. S. losses in Vietnam.

Despite the almost complete surprise and heavy losses, the 1967 cease-fire lines gave Israel the time to mobilize its reserve forces and move to a counter-offensive on both fronts. Those who had advocated for not giving up the territories taken from Jordan, Syria, and Egypt in the Six-Day-War, were now more than ever convinced that only the buffer space provided by the territories had averted catastrophic losses to the civilian population.

And so, in the 1970s and 1980s, the territorial infrastructure was created for a "new Jewish society" of national religious settlers in "Judea and Samaria." The younger generation of the National Religious Party, operating in a youth branch called "*B'nei Akiva*" ("Sons of Rabbi Akiva), became the educational incubators of this movement. A few decades later, they would include more than half of the religious settlers in the West Bank and among its young leaders a young Naftali Bennett.

Municipal and security issues and the need to have a political arm moved the residents of the territories to create a sort of parliament. In 1980 the umbrella organization of Israeli municipal councils in the West Bank territories of **Y**ehuda (Judea), **Sh**omron (Samaria), and Aza (Gaza) was created under the acronym "YeShA." In addition to municipal and security issues, the Council serves as the political arm of the Israeli residents of YeShA, lobbying for their interests with the Knesset and the government.

As stated on their website:

"Since 2016, the Yesha Council helped pass 13 government decisions with the total budget of 30,000,000 USD.
The Council carries on public relations campaigns for the region and invests in activities that support their goals."

"Yesha Council Strategic Objectives
· To secure the borders of the State of Israel
· To safeguard Israel's strategic expanses–between the Jordan River and the Mediterranean Sea
· To ensure Israel's right to the Land by strengthening Israeli settlement in Judea, Samaria, and the Jordan Valley."

Yesha Council Goals
· Application of Israeli sovereignty in the area
· One million Israelis living in Judea, Samaria, and the Jordan Valley
· The development of roads, transportation, water, electricity, and economic infrastructures

·To double the number of tourists from all over the world and all religions
·To prevent the establishment of a Palestinian state between the Jordan River and the Mediterranean Sea."

Our Challenge
·Construction and development of infrastructures in Israel are based on regional planning and national master plans (TAMA).
·Despite the continually growing and developing Israeli settlement of Judea, Samaria, and the Jordan Valley, these areas have not been included in TAMA plans for over 50 years.
·Without master plans for the area, Palestinian and European initiatives are taking root, thus endangering the continuation of the Zionist enterprise.
·Our aim is to create master plans for the area to enable and ensure sustainable settlement."[55]

Besides its content, it was significant that the Council's declarations contained no references to mitzvahs, God, redemption, or the Bible. Its vocabulary belonged to politics alone: the council's main goal, said the document, was applying Israeli sovereignty to all regions of the Land of Israel.

This new "secular" rhetoric was born out of the need to unite the supporters of Greater Israel against the prospect of territorial compromise about to be implemented in Sinai. However, it would be a mistake to assume that this was not a faith-based initiative because activists and municipal heads rather than rabbis led the

YeShA Council, and loaded religious terms were avoided.

Like Bennet, Dani Dayan, who had become rich in the software business, had gone into politics as Secretary-General of the Tehiya political party. In 2007 he was elected chairman of the YeShA council. A self-declared "completely secular, even a liberal person" Dayan "sincerely believe that without Hebron, and all it represents from a historical and cultural point of view, we are a shallow people." Three years later, he would recruit 38 years old Naftali Bennet to become the director-general of the then 350,000 settlers YeShA Council.

Under the pressure of US President Barak Obama, Prime Minister Benjamin Netanyahu had become the first Israeli prime minister to announce a freeze on settlement building officially. Though supposed to be only a temporary ten months freeze, some believed that Obama had forced Netanyahu to make a significant shift on the Palestinian issue. Bennett was tasked to lead the fight to cancel the construction freeze and reinforce the settlement enterprise.

> *"As Netanyahu leads Israel toward peace talks, he "is being bullied into doing something that is against Israel's self-interest, and he knows it, but he feels that he doesn't have a choice,"*

Bennett told the American Jewish News Media the Forward, at the time.

> *"Jerusalem and Judea and Samaria are the heart and soul of Israel,"* he said. *"If Israeli control of these areas is compromised, they will become bases for Iranian-funded radicals, and Israel will have "a soulless body, which I think will not survive in the long term."*[56]

Bennett's objective was to form a solid domestic lobby composed of non- settlers living in new suburbs or people with an economic interest in the West Bank.

> *"We saw in Gush Katif how quickly houses can be demolished, and that's why there's a lot more outreach and connection to the Israeli public,"* he said. He added: *"There was the disengagement, and Yesha's main mission today is to re-engage."*

In this "re-engagement," by which he means attempting to win over other Israelis to the settlers' side, having a non-settler heading the Yesha Council sends an important message, he said."[57]

In July 2011, a Facebook protest about the cost of living in Israel led hundreds of people to establish tents in the Rothschild Boulevard in the center of Tel Aviv. The act soon gained momentum, attracting hundreds of thousands of protesters from various socio-economic and religious backgrounds who protested against the continuing rise in the cost of living and the deterioration of public services such as health and education.

Bennett and Shaked also sided with the young people of Tel Aviv in their socioeconomic struggle and threw their support behind them.

True, Bennett was a right-wing figure who served as CEO of the settlers' Yesha Council, but he claimed that he wanted to broaden the settlers' engagement with other parts of Israeli society. "In the organizer's minds, this was a broad-based social movement that cut across age, ethnicity, geography, and political affiliation.
Unity was paramount, so any talk about divisive "political" issues like the peace process or West Bank settlement was avoided.[58]

Following the original philosophy of the Zionist movement in which he grew up, Bennett was looking for inclusivism.
He understood that the council's success required higher levels of cooperation between religious and nonreligious activists dedicated to the practical political task of incorporating the whole Land of Israel into the State of Israel.

His aim was not to defeat the country's liberal-left elite but to win them over. The confrontational attitude of the old guard, in his opinion, was too divisive and ended by alienating the Tel- Aviv bourgeoisie.

His critics, however, felt he was building his own personal brand.

Then there was also the matter of his living in a Tel-Aviv suburb.

> "He's like a U.N. spectator — he's an outsider," said Daniella Weiss, former mayor of Kedumim in the West Bank and an icon of hard-line settlers. She likened the Yesha Council's choice to an army selecting "a chief of staff who hasn't been in a large battle." A settler leader "has to know what it's like having sheep and goats, and one Shabbat afternoon, Arabs coming and stealing them," she said."[59]

Bennett claims that his place of residence is an advantage. One of his main priorities is to ensure that a mass evacuation, like that which accompanied the Gaza disengagement of 2005, will not happen again. He said the disengagement was able to occur because settlers failed to galvanize mainstream Israel against it.

> *"The folks that live in Judea and Samaria are living there, many of them, as a mission both from a spiritual sense and from security reasons,"* he said. *"Judea and Samaria, from their perspective, is not about them and their house and what will happen. It's about am Yisrael; therefore, there's nothing strange about having a CEO living in Ra'anana — it's all one Israel."*[60]

Though Bennett shared the ideas of the old Council's leadership, the difference in their approaches was too big. The council's veterans tired of his media stunts and rebranding exercises fired him after a short stint.

Oded Revivi, mayor of the Efrat settlements and foreign envoy for the group, remembers Bennett's stint as uneventful and ineffective. "I can't say that during this period, there was a single specific goal that was completed," he said in an interview."[61]

Chapter 4

Habayt HaYehudi

> "The crazies are no longer in the forefront. The settlement project is settled. And now, it has gone from a radical avant-garde to a middle-class establishment. They are no longer about messianic fantasy." [62]

Jewish religious Orthodoxy is not unanimous when it comes to the State of Israel. Attitudes in this camp range from radical delegitimating the State to virtual sanctification of the land and its institutions.

All Orthodox Jews, however, share in common the premise that God has promised to restore his people to the land of Israel in its biblical borders and agree that the Torah, as interpreted by Orthodox sages, is the existential reason and task on earth of the Jewish people.

They differ on whether the redemption will be brought solely by spiritual repentance and ritual observance or in combination with political and military activity.

In 1902 Orthodox Jews concerned about the attacks of those who, waiting passively for Divine Providence to send the Messiah, opposed Jewish sovereignty in the land of Israel and wanted to prevent a secular Israel, formed the *Mizrahi* political party. Its objective was to enable religious Jews to become partners in building a Jewish state while acting as a watchdog within the Zionist movement.

From the start, the party functioned as the leading spokesman for the religious camp. Its focus was the preservation of the status quo on religion and state, the exemption of Orthodox girls from military service, assurance that kashrut would be observed in the dining facilities of the army and other state institutions, respect for the Sabbath, nurturing of the national religious education system, the religious kibbutz movement, and social welfare.

As time went by, *Mizrahi*- now rebranded *Mafdal*[63] -which had served as a member of all the *Mapai*[64]- and *HaAvoda* led governments[65]- migrated steadily rightward.

In 1976 *Mafdal* broke ranks with *HaAvoda*. One year later, it joined the first right-wing led government formed by Menahem Begin.[66] And, then, considering it a divinely-ordained duty, it embraced the religious settlement movement that encouraged Jews to live in the territories, especially those of the West Bank.

Over time demographic changes unavoidably shifted the balance of power in the religious camp, precipitating the *Mafdal* on a downward spiral path. Mostly, however, the party was shooting itself on the foot by increasingly representing extremist factions instead of the entire national religious population as it was its foundational principle.

From having had as many as 12 seats in the *Knesset* during the first decades of the state, by 1981, it had lost half of its electoral strength. Twelve seats now became six and, then, no more than four.

Searching to reinvigorate the party and increase its power in the Knesset, the *Mafdal* changed leadership in 2002. Instead of the traditional venerable rabbis, Effi Eitam- a one-time non- religious kibbutznik, was appointed the party's head.

A former infantry commander with a controversial military career, Eitam had resigned from the army when he was denied General rank. He didn't shy from expressing bold views to say the less:

> "The fact that we are not sitting on the Temple Mount and not sitting in *Eretz Israel* is the point of darkness that embodies all the evil, all the presumptuousness and the wrong of the world."[67]

He would confess to Jeffrey Goldberg from "*The New Yorker*" magazine that he believed innocent men were among the Palestinians but collectively guilty. "We will have to kill them all. I know it's not very diplomatic. I don't mean all the Palestinians, but the ones with evil in their heads. Not only blood on their hands but evil in their heads. They are contaminating the hearts and minds of the next generation of Palestinians."[68]

> "I don't call these people animals. These are creatures who came out of the depths of darkness. It is not by chance that the State of Israel got the mission to pave the way for the rest of the world, to get rid of these dark forces militarily."

Coalition politics made room for Eitam to be Minister of Housing and Construction in Israel's thirtieth government under Ariel Sharon. Soon, however, his extremism put him on a collision course with Sharon's disengagement plan. Sharon had proposed Israel unilaterally withdraw from Gaza, which it had occupied since 1967.

On 13 September 2004, the *Mafdal* party's "center"[69] voted on a choice between Effi Eitam's proposal to immediately resign from Sharon's government and Zevulun Orlev's proposal to stay in under specific circumstances qualifications.[70] Orlev, also a member of the *Mafdal*, serving as Minister of Welfare and Social Services, won 65% of the vote over Eitam's proposal. Refusing to heed the party's decision, Eitam's quit the government, making room for Orlev to take over the party.

A co-president of the international Mizrachi movement, which the *Mafdal* represented in the political arena, Orlev had written an article in the weekly Hebrew Journal Olam Katan, calling for the rebuilding of the Temple in Jerusalem. In it, he had acknowledged that to remove the "religious and political impediment to his plan, that is the al-Aqsa Mosque, and Dome of the Rock atop the Temple Mount would mean that the "billion-strong Muslim world would surely launch a world war." It will be necessary to defeat no-confidence motions, to overcome the hostile, left-wing, secular media, and to ignore eye-rolling economists who will say it's a waste of public funds," he wrote.

Orlev was mindful that the passage of a law would be necessary to protect the Third Temple project from accusations of discrimination, inequality of women in the Temple service, and animal cruelty in the offering of sacrifices. [71]

By 2009, the *Mafdal* had merged with the *Moledet* Party and changed its name to "*Bayit ha-Yehudi*" (Jewish Home), a move that, however, didn't shield it from its downward path.

It was amidst this political climate that Bennett, weighing his options for an elected position, seemed to have appeared virtually out of nowhere.

Having been part of Netanyahu's inner circle, he certainly had clout and connections to run within the Likud party. However, the talk in the street was that the hostility of the prime minister's wife was as intense as was her power and that all Likud doors were closed to him.

Another version asserts that Bennett knew he would always be nothing more than Netanyahu's underling, doomed- like generations of religious Zionist leaders before him- to serve at the pleasure of a strong and secular leader.

Willing to gamble that the tides were turning, that there were enough secular Israelis who found his faith and convictions much more appealing than anything else on offer that election year, Bennet decided to challenge Orlev at the *Mafdal*'s primaries in November 2012

He framed the campaign in terms of a contest between the old and the new. Here was the 40 years old successful high-tech entrepreneur challenging the veteran 60-something national-religious politician Zevulun Orlev.

Working with Moshe Klughaft, his campaign director, Bennett came up with a slogan that would become under different guises the distinctive theme through all his future drives:

"Something New is Happening."

And for a good reason, Bennett has been an advocate for change through all his endeavors, business, military, political, economic, and religion. After overtaking Orlev in a landslide with more than two-thirds of the vote,[72] Bennett launched himself with enthusiasm to the task of changing the way things were.

He went vigorously after the under 30- first-time voters registering new members to the party. He avoided delving too much into its right-wing message attracting a 40 percent non-religious membership at the election to appeal beyond Orthodox Israelis.[73]

As Hartman Institute Fellow and former executive editor of "*The Jerusalem Post*," Amotz Asa-El noted:

> "The first to realize sectarianism's futility was Naftali Bennett. The nominally Orthodox politician who hired a lesbian press secretary and, unlike the rabbis around him, shook women's hands, sought all along a formula to break loose of the sectarian bind.[74]
>
> "The rabbis, who in recent years stood up to defend religious soldiers who boycotted ceremonies where women sang, were now forced to deal with a political leader who posted a video of a girl singing on Facebook for his thousands of followers. He was filmed on television hugging a woman who is not his wife, and worse, he declared publicly that while he consults rabbis, he does not take orders from them. This was a radical departure to the practice of his predecessors over the past 20 years." [75]

"We want to go into the Knesset," Bennett said, *"as the messengers of all Israelis, whether they're Haredi, whether they're religious, nonreligious, whether they're Arabs or Druze. When I wake up as a potential servant of this country, I'm going to think every day about everyone. I'm not going to help a specific sector. And people believe us because I mean it. I*

> *profoundly mean it. When I think about Judea and Samaria, I don't for a moment think I'm representing them as a sector. They're not a sector. I live in Ra'anana[76]. I need Judea and Samaria, and people in Tel Aviv need Judea and Samaria. And people are fed up with special interests and sectorial way of thinking."* [77]

In an interview on *"Time"* magazine conducted by Karl Vick, Bennett said:

> *"We have secular, we have religious for the first time in our party's history – the party predated Israel. It was founded over 100 years ago. For the first time in history, we have a non-religious candidate, in fact, a woman, her name is Ayelet Shaked."* [78]

Shaked, who had been selected to serve as a member of the *Likud*'s Central Committee in January 2012, had resigned to join *Habayit HaYehudi*. She received the highest number of votes in the party primary, placing her behind only Bennett and Construction Minister Uri Ariel. She became the only secular *Knesset* Member of the party and, at age 38, the poster child for *Habayit HaYehudi*'s efforts to reach beyond its Orthodox base. The objective was to appeal to a broader group of voters and "to overcome stereotypes of settlers and their supporters as being religious, gun-toting fanatics."[79]

Bennett was carrying out an internal coup in the very heart of the religious community. In doing so, however, he has continuously been doing nothing more than following the script of the spiritual founder of the National Religious Party, Rabbi Abraham Yitzchak Ha-Cohen Kuk.

In the first third of the twentieth century,[80] Rabbi Kuk tried to bridge the division between believers and nonbelievers. He became the saint and prophet of the liberal wing of Orthodoxy, which identified itself wholeheartedly with the Zionist enterprise, recognizing as their brothers in spirit and destiny the zealous nationalists who denied the sanctity of the Torah."[81]

In the Israel of the 1960s, he became the idolized spiritual guide of religious Zionists when his words were interpreted to declare that when as many Jews as possible would fulfill the single commandment to "settle the holy land," the Messiah will appear to redeem "his people" politically and theologically.

Bennett's strategy succeeded. In the 2013 elections for the 19th Knesset, *Habayit HaYehudi* received twelve *Knesset* seats, the best showing in the history of a religious Zionist party. It became the fourth largest party in the *Knesset*, just behind *HaHavoda*- which had been the main force behind the creation of the state under David Ben-Gurion and dominated the early decades of its politics. Almost overnight, the 40-year-old software tycoon had become a serious political force.

Netanyahu and then Foreign Minister Avigdor Lieberman had joined their two parties, *Likud* and *Yisrael Beiteinu,* to run on a joint ballot in that general election. Contrary to expectation, the two secular right win parties received 11 fewer votes than combined both parties had received before the election. Some in Netanyahu's party blamed Bennett's rise on the *Likud's* decision to merge with Avigdor Lieberman's far-right *Yisrael* Beitenu. As a result, they said, disaffected voters switched to Bennett."[82]

Though it would have been natural to ask *Habayit HaYehudi* in the coalition, Netanyahu did all he could to keep Bennet out of his government. As Mazal Mualem writing for "*Al-Monitor,*" said at the time."

> "The Netanyahus have had plenty of feuds and accumulated plenty of enemies during Bibi's political career, but the conflict with Bennett was the most bitter. Sara Netanyahu regards her husband's former chief of staff as the man who tried to soil her reputation by leaking stories to the press and who slammed the door on his way out when he finally left his position. Worst of all, Bennett never tried to mend fences or apologize throughout the entire election campaign. Instead, he made matters worse by joking at her expense on at least two talk shows."[83]

Netanyahu tried everything. After failed negotiations with *HaHavoda* leader Shelly Yachimovich and having worked an agreement with Tzipi Livni, the leader of *Ha'Tnuah*,[84] a new centrist party, Netanyahu was still short of the necessary seats to form a government.

The next option was another new party, *Yesh Atid*[85], led by Yair Lapid, Israel's most recognizable TV anchor. Considered a voice of secular centrists, the ultra-Orthodox vetoed him. This had put Netanyahu in a bind.

Bennett had met Lapid earlier during the series of tours of the West Bank he had organized while CEO of the YeShA Council. Lapid, then a famous journalist for the *Yedioth Ahronot* newspaper, was hosted on Bennett's private tour of the region. The chemistry between them was instantaneous.

Years later,[86] while covering one of the primary debates between Bennet and Orlev, Hoffman Gil, a reporter for the *Jerusalem Post,* kept the conversation with Bennet continue informally for a long time after the event with Bennett.
The candidate asked Gil if he had met Yair Lapid, who had entered politics three weeks earlier. Gil answered that, as a matter of fact, he met the former anchorman at his Tel Aviv home. Bennett was eager to know his impression of him. At the end of the conversation, Bennet asked for Lapid's phone number.

At the beginning of February 2013, "*Maariv-Makor Rishon*" broke the story that a united front between the Lapid and Bennett parties had been in the making and that they would sit in a Netanyahu government either together or not at all.

Netanyahu could hardly believe that two novice politicians were trying to manipulate him. He was convinced that the old-timers within the party would force Bennett to capitulate and go back on his alliance with Lapid.

According to *"Al-Monitor's Israel Pulse"* columnist Ben Caspit, Netanyahu put out separate feelers to each to gauge whether their mutual commitment was ironclad. "You really won't join me without Naftali?" he asked Lapid, who answered in the affirmative, as did Bennett when Netanyahu put the question to him. Without them, he did not have the required majority.

Hands tied, Netanyahu had no choice but to override his wife's veto and open talks with Bennett. All the while Bennett's position had hardened. He and Lapid now headed the two largest coalition parties in Netanyahu's government.

Bennett had honed his negotiating skills during his years in high-tech, and, novice politician or not, he was ready for this moment. The gives-and-takes had allowed him to gain several key ministerial positions for his party. Among them, he landed for himself the job of Minister of Trade, Industry & Labor, Minister of Religious Services, and Minister for Jerusalem and Diaspora Affairs.

Naftali Bennett is the son of fifth-generation Americans. His maternal grandparents immigrated to the United States from Poland two decades before World

War II. His father's forebears were already in America in the 19th century.

> *"My dad and mom grew up in San Francisco in the fifties, sixties, went to Berkeley; they were very left-wing. In the sixties, my dad was arrested in a sit-in in San Francisco at a hotel that wouldn't hire black people."* [87]

His parents were active reform Jews, members of congregation Emanu-El in San Francisco. After the Six-Day War ended, they emigrated to Israel and volunteered to work at Kibbutz Dafna near the Lebanese border in Upper Galilee.

According to Bennett, his parents *"didn't like the socialist, communal stuff; it wasn't for them."* Naftali's father took a job promoting the Technion, Israel's leading science and engineering university, and the family went to Montreal. During the Yom Kippur War, Jim Bennett flew back to Israel to join his reserve unit in the Golan and stayed with it for several months. Mrs. Bennett then followed her husband back to Israel with their three sons.

Before taking over his seat in the Knesset, Bennett, who held U.S. citizenship as the son of American citizens, renounced his U. S. citizenship.

He entered the highest levels of Israeli politics equipped with the practices and thinking of a successful high-tech entrepreneur, the training and experience of an elite commando officer, and the ethos of the religiously observant Jew. His cultural legacy provides him with a radically different working approach and mindset to most other Israeli politicians. [88]

One of his first projects was his "Singapore Financial Plan," aiming to double the quality of life in Israel. He would do this, he said, by, among other things, "*slashing taxes, Reagan style.*"[89]

He underlined the importance of the marketplace as the engine of wealth in his program by recalling President George W. Bush after the 9/11 terrorist attacks on New York and Washington when "*he told the public to go out and shop. Very patriotic.*" He declared admiringly. [90]

Then, referring to the part of his plan to integrate Israel's most marginal citizens: the *Haredim*[91] and Arabs, he said:

> "*I actually learned a lot from President Obama. People don't get it. It's not about Facebook or Twitter. It's about talking straight and being willing to dive into the most sensitive issues and talk about them honestly. One of the things I learned from him is his famous race speech in the previous campaign, which I thought was a work of art, to take an issue that has always been taboo and talk about it. So, I did this, for instance, with, for example, the Haredim issue, and I think in a way that no one else attempted.*

You know the populist thing is to say, we need a law tomorrow, and all of them will join the army, period. But that's nonsense."[92]

In June 2013, after being appointed Minister of Religious Services, Bennett met with the Rabbinical Assembly of the Conservative movement in Israel's Knesset. He expressed gratitude and appreciation for the movement. He called for all Jewish streams "to engage in dialogue, not through a feeling that someone is above someone else because nobody is better than the other, but in partnership."[93]

In August, Bennett managed an end to the run around the debate over a controversial compromise proposal by Jewish Agency Chairman Natan Sharansky to resolve the long-standing dispute between the ultra-Orthodox-dominated Western Wall Heritage Foundation, which administrates the central Western Wall plaza (the *Kotel*), and those demanding access to Judaism's holiest site for liberal Jewish groups and customs."[94]

He ordered the construction of a platform for egalitarian services adjacent to Robinson's Arch, an archaeological site at the southern edge of the wall. "The guy came and said, 'Well, let's bring it to the government for approval.' I said, 'No, just go build the thing,'" Bennett recalled. "Within six days, it was up, and now we have an egalitarian pluralistic plaza. Everyone can go, no questions asked."[95] When asked what his orthodox constituency thinks about the move,

Bennet responded: "I'm not sure it's the popular decision, but it's the right decision. I'm not focused just on my own voters, but on all Jews."[96]

In the immediate months after taking the three Israeli ministries, Bennett pushed through legislation to give Israeli couples more freedom in choosing which rabbi officiates at their wedding. Under the same breath, however, *Habayit* demanded and got the right to veto any laws that would change the status quo on religious issues.

In 2013 workers at Kibbutz Ein Hashlosha, which sits on the border with Gaza, heard digging underground and called in the Israel Defense Forces (I.D.F.). A week later, officials announced the discovery of a massive tunnel located some 50 feet below the surface. It ran a mile and a half from the village of Abbasan Al-Saghira, in the Gaza Strip, and ended under, the kibbutz's doorstep. Almost a year later, another tunnel was uncovered. This one penetrated three times farther into Israel.

Two months after discovering the latest tunnel, on June 12, 2014, yeshiva students Eyal Yifrach, Naftali Frenkel, and Gilad Shaar were kidnapped at the bus stop at the settlement of Allon Shvut in Gush Etzion, in the West Bank. It didn't take long for prime minister Netanyahu to announce that the kidnappers were identified as members of the terrorist organization *Hamas* based in Gaza.

While the Israeli army was active in search operations in the West Bank, trying to find the kidnapped teenagers, rockets flew from Gaza into Israel. This provoked the Israeli air force to respond with retaliatory raids.

Eventually, on 30 June, search teams found the bodies of the three missing teenagers in a field northwest of Hebron. They had been shot dead ten times shortly after their abduction. Salah al-Arouri, one of the founders of Hamas's military wing, would eventually say at a conference of the International Union of Islamic Scholars in Istambul[97]- Turkey that Hamas's armed wing, the Izz ad-Din all- Qassam Brigades, was behind the kidnapping and the murder.[98]

On the night the teens' bodies were found, Bennett- a minister in the government and a member of the Security Cabinet- suggested to Netanyahu to launch a ground operation to destroy the tunnels. This, he argued, would be a response to Hamas for the kidnapping and murder and a way to remove the threat to communities near Gaza. Netanyahu wouldn't have it.

However, seven days later, Israeli jets bombed a tunnel that began in Rafah, in the southern Gaza Strip, and exited near Kibbutz Kerem Shalom, killing seven members of Hamas, who were trapped inside. Highly placed government sources feared these operatives were the first wave.

Hamas considered the men who died in the tunnel bombing to be among its most elite, warning publicly, "The enemy will pay a tremendous price." Effectively the next day, all hell broke loose, with *Hamas* firing some 150 rockets indiscriminately in a single day over civilian Israeli territory.

Over the next ten days, *Hamas* would send another 1,500 more. The Israeli air force and navy, all the while, would pound military sites in Gaza with little letup. Israel defense minister Moshe Yaalom, a former chief of staff, would define the goal of the Gaza operation- named "Operation Protective Edge"- "to bring down to zero the fire and attacks out of Gaza."

Though troops and some tanks were gathering around the border with Gaza, justice minister Tzipi Livni expressed Israel's reluctance to conduct a ground operation.

Yaakov Amidror, a former major general and national security adviser said that Israel responded in force after Hamas had done so overnight. "If we don't find a solution through this exchange of fire, and Hamas won't understand what we can do, we'll have no other choice than to do the big operation that we don't want to do today," he said. Israeli public opinion was more supportive of a major military action than the prime minister or the government, "which is soberer," he said. "Israeli public opinion is not only behind the government but is pushing the government."[99]

One of those pushing from inside the government for a most robust response was Bennet. He realized that what differentiated this conflict from the previous one in 2008 was that most sites used to fire rockets were concealed underground. Operatives were able to move through an extensive tunnel network from the insides of homes to launch sites and back again, remaining unseen and hard to reach. He pressured Netanyahu, then-Defense Minister Moshe Yaalon, and army chief Benny Gantz, demanding an offensive against Hamas terror tunnels leading into Israel.

Through his contacts in the army, Bennett had learned that Military Intelligence and the Shin Bet security service knew the existence of 32 tunnels. However, they only had a general plan and no specifics for dealing with them.

On July 18, 13 armed Palestinians emerged from one of the tunnels some 250 meters inside Israel, in an open area two kilometers from Kibbutz Sufa in the Eshkol Region. Spotted by sensors and realizing that they had been discovered, they attempted to run back through the tunnel but were struck by Israeli aircraft. The attack, in line with a series of others, thwarted over the past ten days, including two infiltration attempts from the sea near Kibbutz Zikim, a tunnel near Kerem Shalom, and a drone attack earlier that week, forced the cabinet to approve a ground offensive intended to neutralize the tunnels.

Bennet claimed that only because of his intervention was an action against the tunnels approved. "I pushed for this thing," he said.

Bennett's office issued a statement saying:

> "Minister Bennett's actions during Operation Protective Edge, at the height of the operation against the tunnels, saved the lives of residents of Netiv Ha'asara and Nahal Oz. For two long weeks, as the minister frequently demanded that the tunnels be destroyed, other political factions halted the operation or irresponsibly dismissed the value of the tunnel threat, which left residents of the south exposed to terror attacks. Such behavior is appropriate, even required, of a member of Israel's cabinet. Minister Bennett's demands that the tunnels be dealt with did not come to him from astrologers, but rather from touring the field and meeting with various security and intelligence experts." [100]

The tension between Bennett and other members of the Security Cabinet continued throughout the war. It was clear that Bennett knew tiny details from intelligence reports and operational plans, which he hadn't received through approved channels. This worried Defense Minister Ya'alon, who felt that the amount of information in Bennett's hands wasn't available to other top people except Netanyahu and himself.

A senior official in the *Habayit Hayehudi* party would address the issue in this way:

> "Bennett went to the staging area every two or three days. He's proud of it; he doesn't deny

there were meetings and that he had information from officers on the ground. But there wasn't any other choice. This information wasn't given to the cabinet. He didn't get it in any other way. Bennett is proud of that. It's only thanks to this information and Bennett's frequent demands in the cabinet that the security establishment was prodded toward effective action against the tunnels. If it were up to Ya'alon, no significant action would have been taken." [101]

As Operation Protective Edge began to wind down in late July, Bennett criticized Prime Minister Benjamin Netanyahu's goal in the fighting, which Bennett said should have been "to destroy Hamas" rather than addressing the threat posed by the tunnels." [102]

"The tunnels are not the root of the problem. They are a means for Hamas to carry out their strategy of destruction," said Bennett, adding, "What should be done? Name the target: demilitarization of Gaza, like Judea and Samaria. No rockets, no tunnels. The IDF must be given a clear objective — make that a reality."

On February 28, 2017, State Comptroller Yosef Shapira released the state's report on "Operation Protective Edge." He points to the fact that from the cabinet's establishment on March 18, 2013, until March 23, 2014—the cabinet held no discussions aimed at setting strategic goals concerning Gaza." [103]

Chapter 5

Bennett's Liberal Nationalism

After having "done more than 500 parlor meetings and conferences," Bennet contends that what he keeps on seeing is that 80 percent of the issues that concern Israelis are domestic. Just 15 to 20 percent are about the Palestinian issue.

> *"Everyone's exhausted and fed up with it. The younger folks, because they're young, they're still willing to talk about it. They've not spent the past 30 years discussing this unsolvable thing. But anyone who's 35 and older, screw it, just tell me how I can finish the month without debt and how I can buy a house one day."* [104]

Bennett tells about a friend from military service who suffered a shrapnel wound close to his spine — near his backside. The doctors told his friend that they could operate, but he'd run a severe risk of paralysis to his lower limbs. Alternatively, the friend could learn to live with an unpleasant but manageable problem.

The medical choice was clear, Bennett said. And the choice facing Israel is as clear as well: Rather than try to solve an unsolvable conflict with the Palestinians and risk catastrophe, Israel should opt for limited and practical measures to manage the reality in the West Bank. Israel, Bennet argues, should devote its energy to domestic problems, not to unsolvable problems. It is not surprising then to hear Bennett announce at every opportunity since his taking office as Prime Minister in

June 2021 that *"There will be no diplomatic process with the Palestinians."*

That the Palestinian problem is unsolvable, according to Bennett, is

> *"because we don't have a partner"*[105] *The national conflict between the State of Israel and the Palestinians is not over land. The Palestinians do not recognize the essence of our existence here, and this will be the case for a long time to come. The Palestinian leaders don't accept the very existence of Israel as a Jewish state. At the end of the day, at the critical moment, every Palestinian leader balks. I'm very skeptical that Abu Mazen [Palestinian President Mahmoud Abbas] will be willing to accept Israel as a Jewish state. I don't think he wants to go down in history as the guy who agreed to have a Jewish state."*[106]

In an interview he gave to "Fathom" journal in the winter of 2017, he explained more in detail this aspect of his thought:

> *Former Prime Minister Ehud Barak offered them [the Palestinians] a state, and they refused.*
>
> *I'd say to those in the international community who are so entrenched in the idea of a Palestinian state that (a) the Palestinians have a state in Gaz, a and they blew it, and (b) after 50 years, at what time do we need to rethink? In*

the high-tech world where I come from, if my employees tried the same solution and failed, again and again, I'd fire them as I'd expect them to have tried to tackle the challenge from a different angle by now! There is an industry around this topic – think tanks, journals, professionals, and academics keep on chewing on the same old failed solution. We're not in Europe; we live in a region with very few democracies, and when we tried this idea out, it blew up in our faces, and no one showed us any sympathy. Then the Israeli public has moved to the Right in recent years isn't due to ideology but rather to reality. As a child in the 1980s, we had peace songs on the radio and in kindergartens, and the Israeli public was conditioned to love and believe in peace. Yet over 1,000 Israelis died in the terrorist attacks during the 2000s, after we pulled out of parts of Judea and Samaria in the Oslo framework. We pulled out of Lebanon in May 2000 with hopes for peace – as neither side has any territorial claims on the other – but we got the Second Lebanon War in 2006. We pulled out of Gaza and did everything we were expected to do – withdrew exactly to the former armistice lines, kicked out the Jewish settlers, took out the army, and handed over the keys to Palestinian Authority President Mahmoud Abbas – and what we've had since is an 'Afghanistan,' a Hamastan; rockets that have killed many, three rounds of wars and an insoluble situation.

> *When we take these examples, people here have zero appetite to turn over additional land of our small country – especially the heart of our country – to people who thereafter will turn it into an 'Afghanistan.' No amount of words, paper, or schemes of bringing in drones or foreign peacekeeping forces will persuade us otherwise".*

Despite his objection to the two-state solution in 2013, he had said that he would not veto a government decision to conduct peace conversations with the Palestinians:

> *"I'm not going to do anything to stop the negotiations because this government wants to progress in that direction. I think talking is fine. I am very skeptical that it will lead to anything,"* he said at the time."[107]

Given the realities he understands, Bennett's position consists in trying to "shrink the conflict." A phrase from Israeli philosopher Micah Goodman's book "Catch-67." [108] In Goodman's words:

> "the West Bank itself cannot be deemed to be "occupied," since Israel took control of it in a defensive war against Jordan. And Jordan itself had seized it in a war—and not a defensive one—against Israel in 1948. Israel is under no obligation, therefore, to return the territories since "a world in which there is no price to pay

for aggression is a dangerous world, one in which bullies don't have to face any risks."

Bennett and Goodman, who have known each other for a long time, have been discussing the feasibility of a situation where opposites could work together. Essential for this proposition to have a working chance is to end the "occupation" of the lives of the land's non-Jewish inhabitants.

A limited arrangement in which Israel would withdraw its military presence as much as possible from most of the territories to grant the Palestinians as much freedom as possible. Still, both Bennett and Goodman acknowledge, Israel needs to continue holding the Jordan Valley as its eastern border to maintain its defensive position in those parts of Israel necessary for its security.

Goodman is, however, sensitive that

"This scheme faces a major obstacle. Many Palestinians fear that agreeing to policies that improve the situation in the territories would only serve to legitimize that situation. Many of them would prefer to continue suffering under the yoke of Israeli military rule—without freedom of movement, economic freedoms, or the freedom to build—rather than surrender their claim to full sovereignty."[109]

The reasons for "shrinking the problem" and not solving it entirely is the best that can be done considering the Palestinian historical track

"When it comes to Palestinian terrorism, Israel's security is based on its forces' ability to foil the formation of terror cells in the West Bank on a daily basis. Their great success stems from Israel's wide-reaching intelligence network in Palestinian towns and villages. To guarantee the effectiveness of this intelligence, Israel needs free military access to every part of the Palestinian autonomous areas. This is not the situation in Gaza. Israel pulled its army out of Gaza and consequently wrapped up most of its intelligence network there. The IDF's ability to stop terror attacks from the Gaza Strip is therefore extremely limited. This mistake must not be replicated in the context of unilateral moves in the West Bank." [110]

Thus, Bennett says, *"instead of fighting about what we can't agree on, I would do a Marshall Plan for Judea and Samaria for everyone."*

Bennett's focus is on security rather than on political theology. "His right-wing ideology, such as it is, isn't his prime motivator." [111] His main preoccupation is that

"On our northern border, we have the most concentrated area of rockets in the region in the hands of Hezbollah (and second on earth after the North Korean-South Korean border)." [112]

In an Op-Ed in "The New York Times," in November 2014, Bennett wrote:

> *"This past summer, Hamas and its allies fired over 4,500 rockets and mortars at Israel, demonstrating once again what happens when we evacuate territory to the so-called 1967 lines and hand it over to our adversaries. Peace is not obtained. Rather, we are met by war and bloodshed."*[113]

> *"In the mid-1990s, we pulled out of Palestinian cities as part of the Oslo agreement. In 2000, the second intifada erupted, and over 1,000 Israelis were killed in attacks carried out by terrorists, many of whom came from the very cities we had evacuated.*
> *When we pulled out of Lebanon in 2000, we saw a significant strengthening of Hezbollah, the Iranian-backed militia. During the second Lebanon war, six years later, Hezbollah fired more than 4,300 rockets at our cities.*
> *And in 2005, we withdrew from the Gaza Strip and handed it over to the Palestinian Authority. We were told that Gaza would turn into the Singapore of the Middle East and that peace would grow out of the greenhouses the Jewish residents had left behind.*
> *Instead, those greenhouses were used to cover up terrorists' tunnels dug across the border into Israeli towns and villages. Gaza quickly turned into a fortress of terror."*[114]

He practically pleads with the world

> *"I want the world to understand that a Palestinian state means no Israeli state. That's the equation."* [115]

Unsympathetic, quickly judgmental, and out-of-context commentators regularly refer to Bennett as "a hard-right Israeli ultranationalist," [116] "the leader of the ultra-nationalist Yamina party." [117] However, the 2021 elections have shown that the religious Zionist camp is hardly of one piece, and all parts do not fit into the same box.

"Bennett isn't a liberal," Micah Goodman says. "He is post-sectarian, a moderate, pragmatic, humanist nationalist. He doesn't belong to a particular Israeli tribe. His patriotism is being open to all Israelis." Still, he is more at home with liberal Tel-Aviv than the West Bank settlement of Kedumim, home of Bezalel Smotrich, head of the *Tkuma* party. He is also far from being at home in Hebron, where Itamar Ben-Gvir, head of the *Otzma* party, lives.

Takuma and *Otzma* are two of the best-known faces of right-wing radicalism in Israel. To gain an insight of where Bennett is situated in the right-wing spectrum, suffice to look at these two examples:

In a 2016 Twitter, for instance, Smotrich wrote:

> "It's natural that my wife wouldn't want to lie down [in a bed] next to a woman who just gave birth to a baby who might want to murder her baby twenty years from now."
> He then added that "Arabs are my enemies, and that's why I don't enjoy being next to them."[118]

Smotrich, at the time of this tweet was a part of the *Habayit-Ha-Yehudi* lead by Bennett.

The then minister of education quoted a passage from the Mishnah, the first major written redaction of the Jewish oral traditions, stating that *"every human created in God's image is favored,"* and stressing in his own words that the text speaks of "every human, Jewish or Arab."

He linked his tweet to a post of his from 2015, where he wrote of a Shabbat he spent alongside his father's hospital bed.

> *"In a hospital, there is no significance to race, religion, skin color, sexual orientation or political views,"* he had written in that earlier post, naming *"Khaled from Umm el-Fahm,"* who lay in the bed adjacent to his father's, as an example. *"Everyone is human, and every human was born in God's image."*[119]

As head of the *Ha Yamin HeHadash* party and while being defense minister at the time, Bennet was under mounting pressure by the *Likud* to include the leader of the *Otzma* party Itamar Ben Gvir, on his

Knesset slate. Noting that Ben Gvir famously keeps a photograph of Baruch Goldstein hanging in his living room, Bennet stated:

> *"As the chairman of the New Right party now running for Knesset, and as a former education minister of the State of Israel, I won't include on my slate someone who keeps a photograph in his living room of a man who murdered 29 innocent people,"* Bennett said.
> *"That's so self-evident that I'm amazed I'm being asked to explain it at all."*

In a *"Times of Israel"* article[120] where it was noted that "He also lashes *Otzma Yehudi*'s support for the "price tag" terror attacks against Arabs, and for the "hilltop youth" violence targeting Palestinians and IDF soldiers, Bennett was quoted saying:

> *"Instead of building, they break. Instead of repairing, they riot. This is an ideology of deep disdain for the State of Israel and its institutions,"* he says of the party. *"We didn't return from the exile to live as wild, lawless militias. That's not right-wing; it's anarchy."*

Bennett had also stated that he is against any settlement building on privately-owned Palestinian land. In cases where this has happened, he said that legal action should be taken against the guilty party — *"either you move the homes or reach an arrangement of compensation like anywhere else in Israel according to Israeli law."*[121]

"After more than two decades of working on a single solution for the Israeli-Palestinian conflict — the establishment of a Palestinian state — it is time to realize that coexistence and peaceful relations will not be obtained through artificial processes imposed on us from above. Instead, I propose a four-step plan.

First, we would work to upgrade the Palestinian autonomy in the West Bank, in the areas mainly under Palestinian control (known as Areas A and B, according to the Oslo Accords). Ideally, this will be done in coordination with the Palestinian Authority.

The Palestinians will have political independence, hold their own elections, select their own leadership, run their own schools, maintain their own social services, and issue their own building permits. They should govern themselves and run their day-to-day lives. Israel should not interfere. Much of this already exists, but we can do better.

This Palestinian entity will be short of a state. It will not control its own borders and will not be allowed to have a military.
Gaza already functions as a state, but the Hamas government in control there is bent on Israel's destruction. As long as Gaza remains on this path, it cannot be a party to any agreement.

The second step will see the massive upgrade of roads and infrastructure, as well as the removal of roadblocks and checkpoints throughout the West Bank. The objective will be to ensure freedom of movement for all residents — Palestinian and Israeli — and to improve their quality of life.
No peace, though, can last without economic viability. So, the third step will be to build economic bridges of peace between Israelis and Palestinians.

In my former career as a high-tech entrepreneur, I saw how diverse people from different backgrounds could learn to work together in pursuit of economic prosperity. Already, there are 15 industrial zones in the West Bank where Israelis work alongside about 15,000 Palestinians. These zones pump about $300 million a year into the Palestinian economy. Imagine what another 15 industrial zones could do." [122]

"I'm open to ideas about how this materializes; it could be a confederation with Jordan, or local municipalities, or a central government. It would encompass full freedom of movement, massive infrastructure investment, the creation of a tourism zone so Christians can enter Haifa, Nazareth, Nablus, Ramallah, Jerusalem, and Hebron without going through roadblocks. We would have joint industrial centers, and we'd be able to create a land port

> *governed by the Palestinians in Jenin that would be connected to Haifa."* [123]

"Israel," he said, should annex "Area C" of the West Bank, where more than 350,000 Israeli settlers live under full Israeli military and civil control. [...] Palestinians in Area C, which makes up 60 percent of West Bank territory, would be offered Israeli citizenship.[124]

> *"We should apply sovereignty in Israeli-controlled areas – known as Area C – and Palestinians living there will become part and parcel of the State of Israel. And since you cannot have two levels of people within the State of Israel, those Palestinians living in Area C – approximately 80,000 people – will be offered full Israeli citizenship, including voting rights. I think most will opt for residency rather than citizenship (like in East Jerusalem), but it's up to them. They can be Israeli citizens, Israeli residents, or Palestinian citizens."* [125]

Though it is difficult for people who live in other parts of the world to think of Bennett as a liberal when it comes to the territories, this aspect of him is seen more clearly when looking at the economy, where he talks about "reviving" Zionism through an infusion of "Jewish values."

> *"A young couple here has no future because you work really, really hard, but it doesn't add up.*

> *You can't get through the month, and you can only dream about owning your own home. The way Israel's economy is run today is not Zionist. It's not Zionist that young couples and older families are in perpetual economic survival mode. Some of them are leaving the country. When Israel becomes a paradise for working people, they'll stay, not only out of Zionism but because it is truly good here.* And Diaspora Jews will come to live here. That is Zionism.
>
> *It's not Zionist that young couples and older families are in perpetual economic survival mode.*"[126]

What is valid for families is also true for businesses and enterprises. He accordingly renamed the Ministry of Trade, Industry, and Labor, where he was appointed in 2013: Ministry of Economy. Whereas the Finance Ministry's task was to deal with the state's economy from a fiscal perspective, it was fundamental to focus his ministry, the Ministry of Economy, on the task of promoting Israel's economic growth, supervising and encouraging trade, assisting research and, developing and, regulating consumer products.

While conscious that private businesses are the engine of economic growth and needless government regulation rather than more, he also understood that the major labor unions, the tycoons, and even the Ministry of Defense monopolies were strangling the economy. In practice, Bennett was repositioning his newly named

Ministry of Economy from being "a virtual lobby for industrialists to be an agent for increasing competition."[127]

> *"If there is one thing I would want to achieve over the next four years, it is to break up the monopolies here and to break the stranglehold the big unions have on the Israeli economy."*"[128]

He applied this same "we are not prisoners" mindset that dominated his attitude towards monopolies by reducing trade with the European Union and increasing trade with emerging markets worldwide.

> *"We still trade with Europe, of course, but we need to diversify, and it's good to be involved now with places with no history of anti-Semitism, where we are just perceived as who we are, not as what others think we did or didn't do 2000 years ago."* [129]

The Economy Ministry began opening new trade attaché offices in Asia, Africa, and South America while closing some trade offices in Europe and consolidating others with offices in neighboring countries.

As part of this process, Bennett opened negotiations with Russia and China on free trade agreements, oversaw continuing talks with India for a free trade agreement, and led economic delegations to China and India.

It was thus clear that his program's objective was not simply to increase revenue but to support vulnerable populations such as the elderly and disabled and to encourage greater integration of Israel's most marginal citizens: the Haredim and the Arabs.

> *"With extremely low labor participation, ultra-Orthodox Jews and Israeli-Arab women have unfortunately slipped into a situation of welfare and poverty. For ultra-Orthodox men, it stems from a refusal to serve in the military and instead to sign up for religious study in yeshivas. For Arab women, it has been the lack of education and a culture in which they are expected to stay at home. Transforming the labor market will not be easy. There is prejudice against both the ultra-Orthodox and the Arab community. Many of the Arab women live far away from main cities where the jobs are; and, in many cases, husbands prefer that their wives stay at home."* [130]

The premise of Bennett's plan is that Israel is successful in innovation, but its economic potential is undermined by poor management and considerable bureaucracy. In exhibit A, he compares Israel with Singapore.

There are several similarities between Singapore and Israel. Both countries are small and densely populated states. Both were founded after World War II. Both have initially been poor and have faced hostilities from their respective neighbors. Singapore's military was modeled after the Israel Defense Forces with the assistance of Israeli military advisors.

After gaining independence, both Singapore and Israel invested heavily in education and technological development. As a result, Singapore and Israel eventually emerged as first-world economies by the end of the 20th century. While Israel became known as the Start-Up Nation, Singapore became a leading financial and technological hub in the global economy.

In 2003- Bennett doesn't stop repeating- Israel and Singapore had a similar GDP per capita. In 2020, however, Singapore's GDP per capita was more than double that of Israel's purchasing power. Bennett attributes the considerable current difference in GDP per capita to Singapore's competent economic management.

Bennett attributes the high cost of living in Israel to regulations and lack of competition.

> *"Things are expensive, very expensive in Israel for many reasons. One of the reasons is our ports. It's a monopoly. They run very poorly. And we have ships that are stuck in the ocean for three or four days or a week, and all that cost is transferred to the products and the consumer. To fix it, you need to create a fair, open market and competition."*[131]

There are three tax systems, says Bennett: Value Added Tax, Income Tax, and National Insurance. It should become a single tax system. People who pay 50 percent would pay 35 percent. To found it, the country needs massive growth, which can also be achieved by slashing corporate tax from 23% to 15%. This will attract the creation of new companies and grow old ones.

Together with cutting taxes, stimulate spending, and aiding vulnerable parts of the population, Bennett emphasizes the need of running Israel competently.

While Israel is known worldwide for its innovative high-tech industry, much of Israel's public sector remains low-tech and bloated. Bennett believes that customer service levels and quality of life in Israel can be dramatically upgraded by introducing effective high-tech management style to Israel's inefficient and bureaucratic public organizations." [132]

> *"In Hebrew, there's no word, no accurate translation, for "competence." We need a word for it, and we certainly need competence."* [133]

Chapter 6

The New Right

> "In one word, that is called putsch, and that makes it impossible to run a government, that makes it impossible to lead a country. Therefore, a short while ago, I instructed the cabinet secretary to issue dismissal letters to ministers Livni and Lapid. Therefore, also due to the necessity to ensure stable and proper conduct of government, I decided to push forward legislation to dissolve the Knesset and go to the election as soon as possible."[134]

On December 2, 2014, prime minister Netanyahu reached the conclusion that he could no longer keep working with the centrist parties in the government coalition he had put together in the 2013 elections. He thus dissolved the Knesset, triggering the need to elect a new government. In a harbinger of things to come, this was the first time in more than five decades that the *Knesset* was dissolved in less than two years after it had been elected.

Netanyahu's move presumed that *Likud* would continue to garner the most votes and that he would succeed in forming a coalition with the nationalist and *Haredi* parties without the need of the centrist parties of Lapid and Livni. Two polls conducted the following day seemed to confirm this. According to a Channel 10 poll, *Likud* would win 22 seats, *Habayt HaYehudi* 17, *Yisrael*

Beytenu 12, the ultra-Orthodox *United Torah Judaism* eight, *Shas* seven. A similar survey by Channel 2 differed only in that it gave *Yisrael Beytenu* 10 mandates instead of 12, but *Shas* with nine instead of seven would compensate for the difference.

For Bennett, the call to new elections meant that he had the opportunity he was looking for to refresh the list of candidates in his party. He felt that the *Habayit Hayehudi* list was in general sectarian and extreme rightist. So, he had taken steps to position himself to effect changes when the time would come.

In early September 2014, the party approved empowering him with greater control over who got to become a Knesset Member. In addition to giving one guarantee spot out of every five for a female candidate, the updated party constitution gave Bennett the right to choose one out of every five candidates on the party list. He was also going to be the one to decide who would get to be a minister.

Bennet had made it clear when he took over the old *Mafdal*- now revitalized since 2012 under his leadership, as *Habyit HaYehudi*- that:

> *"We don't need a religious party anymore. We need to open it up to secular Israelis. We need to restore Jewish identity and strengthen our power in the region."*

It is impossible not to see here a line of thought inspired in the radical interpretation of secular Zionism of who is considered the spiritual father of the *Mizrahi* party, the forerunner of *Habayt Hayehudi*-: Rabbi Abraham Isaac Kuk.

Appointed by the British in 1921 to serve as Palestine's Ashkenazic chief rabbi, Rabbi Kuk provided the religious, intellectual scaffold to do what the Haredim haven't been able or willing to do: have religious law observant Israelis reach those who aren't and vice-versa. In other words, to see the unity of the Jewish people[135].

Rabbi Kuk considered secular Zionists and Orthodox two complementary parts of a higher synthesis.
According to this thinking, the secular Zionist, like the Orthodox, responds to a divine call, although he is not aware of who is calling him. Both, however, are instruments at the service of God.[136]

Bennett, who in a 2019 Facebook post defined his personal religious practice as "Israeli-Jewish," reminds those who want to hear it that he married his wife Gilat, from a secular family and that key people in his party, such as Ayelet Shaked, are secular. In fact, he says, the party attracted a 40 percent non-religious membership in the past election.

Bennett also understood that as long as *Habayit HaYehudi* kept functioning as a sector, it would never become a party, able to replace the Likud and govern the country.

This was clear to the party's members. Member of the Knesset Yoni Chetboun, for instance, commented about Bennet: "He wants to change the Jewish Home into a *Likud* B, and to attract to himself secular right-wing voters. We don't need to be a right-wing secular party, even if that means that tomorrow we don't wake up with 30 seats." [137]

Jumping at the opportunity presented by the call to early elections and the prerogatives he had obtained to place some of the candidates on the party's list, he called on former MTV presenter Eden Harel, who turned his offer down.

But, of course, there was Ayelet Shaked, who ended by scoring another resounding triumph in the primaries, taking the third post in the list of candidates right behind Naftali Bennett and Uri Ariel.

Then he thought about Dr. Anat Roth. She had worked as an aide to *HaHavoda* chief Amram Mitzna and cabinet member Matan Milnai before embracing both religion and right-wing politics. Bennett displaced another female candidate preferred by the party to make room for Dr. Roth. Former *Peace Now* activist took the place of Rabbanit Yehudit Shilat, a pioneer of Orthodox feminism and the wife of a rabbi whom Bennett reportedly saw as too close to right-wing rabbis.

Ultimately, none of the two women made it to the Knesset Rabbanit Shilat, who was placed on the 19th and the last post in the *Habayit Hayehudi* list of candidates captured 1,375 more votes than Dr. Roth, who occupied the 14th post. The whole move, however, created tensions within the party.

Bennet succeeded with his pick of Yinon Magal, the editor of the Walla! Web site, who had admitted in an interview that he smoked marijuana. The *Bayit HaYehudi* chairman, however, was looking for a star that would attract a new and large amount of voters. Without realizing he thus committed one of the biggest blunders of his political career so far.

Bennett had recruited former Beitar Jerusalem striker Eli Ohana, one of Israel's most decorated soccer stars and an icon of the Oriental Jewish community. He placed him in the tenth spot on *Habayit HaYehudi*'s roster, inadvertently creating an internal political tsunami.

Lev Solodkin, the *Habayit Hayehudi* student leader at Tel Aviv University, wrote to Bennett on Facebook: "What does it say about you that you gave an assured spot to someone like Ohana, denying a spot to party members who worked their butts off in the primary?"

According to Solodkin, "I'm not one of the settlers with a military jacket and an Uzi over my shoulder. I'm a secular young man from central Israel. You may lose my friends and me if this man is the best you could come up with for the guaranteed spot." [138]

For the first time since he was chosen as party chairman, Bennett was confronted with wall-to-wall opposition from within his party. Members of the *Knesset* were furious over the fact that an outsider would be pushing out a party member from the opening ten on the party list. They opposed the choice itself.[139]

As Amotz Asa-El pointed out: "the people expected to vote for Ohana were neither Brazilian soccer worshipers nor Californian sunbathers, but rabbis, settlers, feminists, teachers and professionals whose shared appreciation for observance, spirituality, and scholarship is pretty much the opposite of what happens in Israeli soccer stadiums. The stadium is arguably a vestige of ancient paganism, and the modern athlete's popular celebration smacks of idolatry, said Asa-el. This attitude is, of course, debatable, but among observant Jews, it is common. Moreover, observant voters are generally opposed to Israeli soccer's systematic desecration of Shabbat, in which Ohana was a central participant. "How can we be represented by a man who desecrated Shabbat publicly?" asked some of Bennett's critics, citing a famous Talmudic phrase characterizing a Jew gone astray." [140]

Three days after declaring his candidacy, the soccer star was forced to withdraw under exceedingly contemptuous attack.

When the dust settled, Bennett's gambit had backfired, underscoring *Habayt HaYehudi*'s long-standing sectarianism rather than the open-minded spirit. The relationship between Bennett and the religious right had always been an uneasy one. Yai Rosenberg, writing for *Tablet Magazine,* sums up:

"The hip, hi-tech entrepreneur was married to a non-Orthodox Jew, had no problem with LGBT people, and generally presented as more modern in his attitudes than many of the constituents he purported to represent. The settler's rabbis tolerated Bennett because he made a good frontman for their movement. As a yarmulke-wearing hi-tech millionaire who had served in Israel's special forces, he was the embodiment of the religious Zionist dream. But while the party's traditionalists turned to the untraditional Bennett in the hopes that he would win them votes, they did not always give him the latitude to do so."[141]

In any event, the Ohana incident alerted Bennett of the impossibility of achieving national dimension through the parochial constituency of a party such as *HaBayit HaYehudi*.

Though *Habayit HaYehudi* scored only eight seats on the March 17, 2015 elections for the 20th Knesset, former Foreign Minister Avigdor Liberman's bombshell announcement that he would not join the government made Bennett indispensable for Netanyahu to form a coalition. This was the political height for Bennett and Shaked, who had reached the top of their influence due to Netanyahu needing their support. Bennett was thus, appointed minister of education, while Shaked, not yet forty, led the prestigious Justice Ministry."[142]

Chapter 7

Education

> "The camera focuses on a teacher with her back to her students. She writes a formula on the whiteboard and asks, "Who knows what sin α is?" One of the students responds by tossing a paper airplane at the teacher. At first, she demands to see the student's parents. Still, when the teacher picks up the paper airplane, she discovers that the insolent student — who happens to be former President Shimon Peres — wrote the correct answer. "You may amount to something after all," says the teacher with a faint smile."

The TV ad was part of the "Give Five" campaign Bennett had developed as education minister.

During the coalition's discussions in preparation for the 2015 elections, Bennett had demanded from Netanyahu the defense portfolio. As it came to be, *Habayit Hayehudi,* in the end, didn't meet the expectations and received fewer votes than in the previous election, four votes less, in fact. With eight mandates, Bennett could hardly expect the prestigious Defense job and had to change demands. In the past, the *Mafdal* traditionally had requested the education portfolio to benefit the sector's institutions, and Bennett took it as a challenge rather than with disappointment

The "Give Five" campaign was a component of Bennett's ambitious "Startup Nation" strategy. He intended to double the number of students completing five units in mathematics in their matricular exams.

When coming to the ministry, he faced an Israel ranking along with countries such as Germany, Holland, Russia, Spain, and England – with only 9.1% of high-school students completing high-level mathematics studies.

Bennett pushed to move Israel up to the next bracket of 16% to 30%, alongside countries such as Australia, Estonia, Finland, France, Hong Kong, and Sweden.

To encourage students to take the highest-level exams in mathematics, he added 160 classes mainly in the periphery and among schools in the Arab, *Haredim*, and Bedouin sectors – where there were previously no options for higher-level math studies available.

Two hundred sixty-eight education students began training in high-level mathematics education, compared with 73 the previous year.

This was the same year when Israeli President Reuven Rivlin speaking at the annual Herzliya Conference, acknowledged, in what became famously known as the "Four Tribes" that Israeli society was undergoing a profound transformation.

> "This is not a trivial change; it is a transformation that will restructure our very identity as Israelis and will have a profound impact on the way we understand ourselves and our national home," the country's President had said.

President Rivlin spoke about Israel being home to four main tribes sharing the common public space. As evidence of the existence of these tribes, the President brought up that the country has four educational branches: secular, Arab, religious, and *Haredi*.

Children born in the State of Israel are sent to one of four separate education systems. Each system aims to educate the child and form their worldview according to a different ethos or culture, religious belief, or even national identity.

> A child from Beth El [religious settlers], a child from Rahat [Bedouin Arabs], a child from Herzliya [secular Jews], and a child from Beitar Ilit [ultra-Orthodox Jews]— not only do they not meet each other, but they are educated toward a totally different outlook regarding the basic values and desired character of the State of Israel, the President said.

And then he asked:

Will this be a secular, liberal state, Jewish and democratic? Will it be a state based on Jewish religious law? Or a religious democratic state?

> Will it be a state of all its citizens, of all its national, ethnic groups? Tribe, by tribe, by tribe, by tribe."

When the state was formed, Israel decided to be a multicultural society rather than a melting pot. Now, President Rivlin's words addressed the need to create a shared Israeli character- a shared "Israeliness."

It had always been thought that the most severe problem facing the Israeli state education system was budgetary. Yet, the Education Ministry in 2014, before Bennett took over, already had a considerable budget: 44 billion shekels ($11.3 billion), Israel's second-largest budget after the defense. The real challenge, as Yael Tamir- a liberal Education Minister serving between 2006 and 2009 said- was that "there isn't a country in the world that doesn't want to teach some kind of cultural heritage. But the question is when that turns into indoctrination."[143]

Bennett has always maintained that when it comes to the nation's unity, he could bracket his personal preferences to a limit. This would be one of his most significant tests.

Fast behind the "Give Five" campaign, the test for Bennett came when he tried to ensure that 9th through 12th-grade Israeli students taking part in delegations abroad, whether to conferences or international contests in mathematics, science, and technology, represent Israel as its ambassadors.

An 11 study units course consisting of films lasting several minutes was designed.

Bennett spoke on the first unit:

"Israel is a power of doing good to billions of people worldwide. The Arabs vote and are elected to the Knesset; only in Israel is there such democracy. Emphasize this because sometimes they throw out a word like apartheid. What apartheid? The Arab states don't want the tiny Jewish democracy to survive. Those guys sitting in London or the United States must be told that we're the free world's forward outpost in the global campaign against radical Islam."

The course was criticized because it was political, though not necessarily partisan, as its detractors contained. As one of the parents had put it: "Now we have to agree to a blatantly political agenda so that the child can go to a scientist competition."

Then Bennett banned members of the controversial Breaking the Silence NGO from delivering lectures in Israeli high schools. The move came after senior Breaking the Silence members were caught on camera telling diplomats and politicians visiting Israel exaggerated and decontextualized stories, framing Israel as needlessly persecuting the Palestinians."[144]

He removed a play from the list of those subsidized by the state: "A Parallel Time." The work was based on the life of Israeli Arab Walid Daka, who was serving a life sentence for being involved in the abduction and killing of Israeli soldier Moshe Tamam. The play had drawn sharp criticism from the soldier's family and those on the Israeli right who insisted that it should not receive public funding."[145]

He also dropped from the curriculum Dorit Rabinyan's novel on the relationship between a Jewish woman and a Palestinian man. Yet, he decided, as education minister, to award the Israel Prize to author David Grossman.

Born in Jerusalem in 1954, Grossman is one of Israel's most highly acclaimed and widely translated novelists. "He is not just one of the greatest Israeli novelists today," said Bernard Henry Lévy about him.

> "He is not just one of the greatest Israeli novelists today," said Bernard Henry Lévy about him. He is also, along with Amos Oz, A.B. Yehoshua, and a few others, one of the country's moral consciences." [146]

One of the most eloquent and methodical spokespeople of Israel's political left for the past several decades — and especially the last few years vis-a-vis a right-wing government in power- David Grossman has been one of the most prominent cultural advocates of a two-state solution to the Israeli-Palestinian conflict."[147]

"The death of young people is a horrible, shattering waste,"

Grossman has said. His 20-year-old son Uri, a tank commander had died fighting in Lebanon in 2006 in the same war Bennet had served. He was addressing his words at a memorial service for Yitzhak Rabin.

"But not less dreadful," he continued: "is the sense that for many years, the state of Israel has been squandering not only the lives of its children but also the miracle it experienced- the great and rare opportunity bestowed upon it by history, the opportunity to create an enlightened, decent, democratic state that would conduct itself according to Jewish and universal values. A state that would be a national home and a refuge, but not *only* a refuge; rather, a place that would also give new meaning to Jewish existence."

He went on to criticize the country's leaders, saying that they could not "help a nation adrift in such complicate state of affairs."

"Mr. Prime Minister, I am not saying these things out of anger or vengefulness. I have waited long enough so that I would not be responding from a fleeting impulse. You cannot dismiss my words tonight by saying that a man should not be judged at his time of grief. Of course, I am in grief. But more than anger, what I feel is pain. This country pains me, and who you and your friends are doing it. Believe me; your success is important to me because the future of us all depends on your ability to get up and do something."

Grossman then pleaded with Olmert to speak directly to the Palestinian people.

> "Go to them over the head of Hamas," Grossman said to Olmert. "Go to the moderates among them, the ones who, like you and me, oppose Hamas and its ways. Go to the Palestinian people. Speak to their deep grief and wounds, recognize their continued suffering. Your status will not be diminished, nor will that of Israel in any future negotiations. But people's hearts will begin to open a little to one another, and this opening has huge power." [148]

Grossman is the first Israeli to win the Man Booker Prize, often considered the most prestigious literary award in the world after the Nobel Prize for Literature for his novel "A Horse Walks into a Bar."

Having proved that his ministry was not hunting legitimate ideological opposition, Bennett's biggest challenge was to tackle the under-performance in Israeli Arab schools, and the lack of teaching core subjects in the Haredi School System

However, Bennett's biggest challenge was to tackle the lack of teaching core subjects in the Haredi School system.

Arabic-speaking schools serving Muslims, Christians, Bedouin, and Druze students have been historically underfunded, and consequentially, Arab students score far lower than Jews in national standardized exams and are less likely to enter higher education.

Previous education minister Shai Piron-of the centrist *Yesh Atid* party started to confront the issue by devising a five-year plan to increase funding to Israeli Arab schools by a billion shekel (about $260 million)

Minister Piron managed only to implement the first year of the scheme falling upon Bennett to continue with the five-year plan that gave priority funding to Arab schools. Bennett chooses to do so, even at the expense of Jewish children in the state religious-system.

The *Haredi* matter was an altogether different issue. Even in 2021, leaders of the *Haredi* community such as Sephardic Chief Rabbi Yitzhak Yosef define the school core curriculum of math, English, science, and computer studies programs as "nonsense."

Chief Rabbi Yitzhak Yosef had said:

"I myself, did I learn the core curriculum? Did I finish school? Until today I don't have a graduation certificate, not a high school diploma, and not a graduation certificate. Did I miss anything? It's nonsense; the most important thing is our holy Torah."[149]

This position is responsible for some 27% of Israel's *Haredim* students- a total of more than 90,000- to be excused from studying math, science, English, and other critical subjects. The number of students exempts from studying the core curriculum soared by 7,300.

According to the 2020 State comptroller report, only 3% of *Haredim* yeshiva students qualify for matriculation (*bagrut*). Thirty-two percent of first-grade pupils at primary schools are *Haredim*.

Less than half of *Haredi* men are presently in the workforce, the lowest participation level of any identifiable group in Israel – and, tellingly, even far less than *Haredim* in other countries.

The minority who do work tend to populate a vast religious bureaucracy that includes supervisors of the *mikvaot* ritual baths, kashrut food certifications, and other apparatchiks.

Chapter 8

The Comeback Kid

In November 2018, a routine Israel surveillance team of the elite Maglan unit penetrated Gaza secretly to install surveillance equipment.

As Israel military spokesman, Lt. Col. Jonathan Conricus explained:

> "Just as terrorist organizations don't stop to plan, and to harbor weapons and try to strike against Israeli civilians, neither do we in our preparations, in our collection efforts, and in our operations that we conduct in order to mitigate the capabilities of the different terror organizations around us."

The operation, however, was botched resulting, in the death of one of the Israeli soldiers and seven Hamas militants. For the next two days, Israel and Hamas were engaged in one of their heaviest fights since the "Protective Edge" confrontation of 2014.

Prime Minister Netanyahu defied public demand to hit back harder and accepted a deeply unpopular ceasefire with Hamas to prevent another war. Minister Avigdor Lieberman accusing the Prime Minister of "surrendering to terror" resigned.

In so doing, Lieberman left the coalition with a razor-thin, one- seat majority. Bennett saw here a new opportunity to move to a more influential ministry and once again announced his candidacy for the coveted position of Minister of Defense. It wouldn't be. To Bennett's dismay, Netanyahu instead took the position for himself.

Shortly after, the governing coalition opted to disband and call for early election in April 2019. This would be the first in a series of unprecedented four elections in under two years.

As Prime Minister Benjamin Netanyahu's four government in office since May 2015 disbanded three-and-a-half years after its first sitting, Bennett and Shaked felt the time to make a new political move had come. In an announcement that stunned the Israeli political world, on December 28, 2010, Bennett and Shaked announced that they were leaving *Habayit HaYehudi* to form a new party: *HaYamin HeHadash*.

Though Shaked had reservations about leaving the party concerned that striking out on their own might be too risky, Bennett insisted. The tensions within the party had escalated to new heights. Bennett had been taken to the party's internal court several times due to disagreements, but there have also been other factors that pressed his decision.

Bennett and Shaked had clashed several times with Agriculture Minister Uri Ariel and MK Bezalel Smotrich, who headed the intransigent *Tkuma* faction within the *Habayit HaYehudi* party.

> "Bennett and Shaked do not believe they can ever win the leadership of Israel so long as they are associated with a religious party, said Smotrich, and the split was therefore "inevitable."[150]

Bennett had long felt that *Habayit HaYehudi* was not able to influence policy within the Netanyahu government and that the Prime Minister felt religious Zionists were "in his pocket," and that, at the end, they would always go ahead with what he wanted.

Thus, at a press conference in Tel Aviv, Education Minister Naftali Bennett and Justice Minister Ayelet Shaked said they would co-chair the new party, which included religious and secular members.

Both ministers were riding a high political wave, with internal polls showing that the "Bennett and Shaked" brand had a hardcore base of four seats. It was composed of ardent supporters who would follow them to whatever party they chose. The general assessment was that they would walk away from the April 9 election with 8-10 seats.

Bennett and Shaked looked to move with their new party toward the center of secular society. They were convinced that they could provide a home to those religious Zionists who felt that *Habayit HaYehudi* had gone a step too far. They presented themselves as a general right-wing alternative to the *Likud* rather than the sectarian approach of their former party.

Bennett even place football team *Hapoel Beersheba*'s owner Alona Barkat as number three in the list in his attempt to reach out to the periphery town voters.

"Other *HaYamin HeHadash* candidates include Shuli Mualem, an MK with theocratic leanings, and Caroline Glick, who supports annexing the West Bank in its entirety."[151]

After the Central Elections Committee finished counting the final 265,000 ballots from soldiers, diplomats, medical staff, and patients in hospitals, prisoners, and disabled people, *HaYamin HeHadash* had received merely 138, 101 ballots, 1,400 less than the necessary to cross threshold of 3.25 percent of the national vote to qualify for the *Knesset*.

On election night, a photo taken by the chief photographer at *The Jerusalem Post*, Marc Israel Sellem, shows Bennett and Shaked walking down a corridor looking exhausted and downcast. It said everything.

In a telling assessment titled: "How did 2 of Israel's most prominent ministers end up outside the 21st Knesset? Jacob Magid from *The Times of Israel* wrote:

> "Beyond choosing too narrow a target audience in an already fractured national religious camp, New Right's campaign messaging was also quite niche.
> "Shaked will defeat the High Court of Justice, Bennett will defeat Hamas," read the party's

campaign posters, plastered along highways throughout the country.
While many on the right appreciate Shaked for appointing more conservative judges to all levels of Israel's courts and backed her stated goal of passing legislation in the next Knesset that will curb the High Court's power to overturn legislation, this largely elitist issue is dwarfed by the security and socioeconomic concerns many Israelis had in mind when they arrived at the polls."[152]

Shaked and Bennett remained in the government. Theoretically, until kicked out by the new administration, that would result from the April 9th election.

Bennett, handed Shaked the reins of the party, and she quickly moved to try to prevent another failure by seeking to merge *HaYamin HeHadash* with other religious right-wing parties. The ensuing alliance between *HaYamin HeHadash*, *Habayit HaYehudi*, National Union *Tkuma* was named the United Right, later renamed *Yamina*.

This was nothing more than a strategic move for all the parties involved to prevent the dispersion of votes. Bennett assured would-be voters, that the new *Yamina* alliance would be no more than a "technical bloc" solely for the upcoming elections and that the parties would part ways after entering the *Knesset*.

In the April 2019 general election, Netanyahu's *Likud* party had won 35 of the 120 seats in the *Knesset*. This was the party's best result since the 2003 election when it had won 38 seats under Ariel Sharon and its best under Netanyahu.

Though the main centrist opposition party, *Blue and White*, had gathered the same number of votes as the *Likud*, Netanyahu's party was nominated to form a new government by 65 lawmakers from right-wing parties. He was now in pole position in negotiations to form a right-wing coalition.

After weeks of political bargaining however, he didn't succeed to command a Parliamentary majority.

The central sticking point was a military draft law that had created a rift between two parts of Netanyahu's right-wing alliance: the secular *Yisrael Beiteinu* faction and the *Haredi* parties.

Though most Jewish men and women are conscripted at 18 and serve at least two years in the Israeli military, *Haredim* engaged in full-time religious studies had been exempted from compulsory military service.

Statistic from the Israel Democracy Institute showed that *Haredim* made up about 11 percent of Israel's population, creating severe resentment in the country.

In 2017 the Supreme Court had ruled that a mass exemption from military service for ultra-Orthodox Jews was discriminatory and unconstitutional. The court gave the government a year to draw a new law. So, during the last session of the *Knesset*, Avigdor Lieberman, the leader of the *Yisrael Beitenu* party, had introduced a bill that would gradually increase the quota of *Haredi* men in military service and impose penalties and fines if the quota were not reached.

Though the bill was unlikely to change the status quo significantly, neither side in the confrontation backed down. The *Haredim* had 16 lawmakers, so Netanyahu blamed Lieberman, who controlled only five seats in the new *Knesset*, for depriving him of the majority he needed to rule.

Normally, Netanyahu could have reached out to centrists to explore an alternative coalition or at least to force a compromise on the right. But Ganz centrist party *Blue and White* said it would not work with Netanyahu while indicted for corruption. The small center-left *HaHavoda* party rebuffed an approach.

Rather than leave the initiative to pass to Israel's President Reuven Rivlin, who could have asked another lawmaker to try to form a government, Netanyahu opted to push for new elections.

New elections were then called for September 17, 2019

Thanks to Netanyahu's failure to form a coalition, Shaked and Bennett had a new shot at the *Knesset*.

In his bid to secure the next elections, Netanyahu supported the merger of the national religious parties.

However, reports were that Netanyahu was not backing Shaked because his wife "Sara says it is Ayelet who is framing Netanyahu" in the corruption cases against him. A leaked recording can be heard: "Netanyahu wants to include *Habayit Hayehudi* in his next government. But he won't take Ayelet Shaked with him." [153]

The September 17 election was another tight race, with Benny Gantz's *Blue and White* party holding 33 seats against *Likud*'s 32. Both failed to win enough votes to build a coalition with a majority.

President Reuven Rivlin once again asked Netanyahu to form a government, giving him 28 days to try.

For the *Yamina* alliance, however, the election paid off. Winning seven mandates, Bennett regained his seat in the Knesset.

In November, *Yamina* and *Likud* announced that the two would be united as a single faction.

To prevent Bennett from crossing the lines to the rival *Blue and White* party, Netanyahu finally appointed Bennett defense minister in November 2019. He became the youngest defense minister in the history of the state." [154]

On February 10 at a campaign event in the Jordan Valley, Netanyahu said

> "The Blue and White party almost had a government. I made the move at the very last

minute and appointed him defense minister. That's the truth."[155]

Six months later, as the result of a new government arrangement Gantz who had opposed Bennett's appointment, would replace him.

But, now Bennett was in charge of the largest organizational machine in all Israel, the Israel Defense Forces.

When it emerged, that Israel was unprepared to conduct sufficient coronavirus tests, Bennett put the IDF's incommensurable human and technological capacities to deal with the Corona crisis.

As Shlomi Eldar writing for *Al-Monitor,* said about Bennett:

> "He is a person who gets things done. He thinks outside the box and is familiar with the rigid system. So, for example, he knows how to take advantage of the Research Department of Israeli Military Intelligence." [156]

Bennett claimed:

"The Ministry of Health has no real expertise in crisis management. Managing tens of thousands of tests per day is not something they could do. If the coronavirus crisis management is not immediately transferred to the defense

establishment, we will not be able to return to normal! I've been soft-spoken about it until now, but it's a matter of life and death!" [157]

Eldar explained in a segment worthwhile to be quoted somewhat extensively due to its insight:

"The Research Department is charged with analyzing information collected by the intelligence agencies operating on different fronts. Some of the best minds in Israeli intelligence head the department. They are the ones who provide the most up-to-date status reports to the defense establishment in general and decision-makers in particular. These include warnings and threats against Israel now and in the future. Bennett has put this system at the disposal of the health care system to help it collect and analyze data from other countries also dealing with the coronavirus. The working assumption is that people in intelligence have the ability and means to sift through data and respond to the queries of senior staff in the health care system.

An army spokesperson revealed this inter-ministerial cooperation to win the military admiration and signal to the political leadership that the well-greased defense system offers a lot. The military can and does contribute well beyond deploying soldiers to patrol the streets to help the police enforce closure orders in towns and cities.

> "An unidentified senior officer in the Research Department who spoke to Ynet explained the advantages of using the Research Department.
>
> "The leaders of the health system came and told us that they were used to waiting a month, a month and a half even, for an answer to their queries, but when they asked us, we gave them an answer in ten minutes." He went on to say that a joint center for the Ministry of Health and Military Intelligence had been set up in Sheba Hospital and is now operating as a war room in the battle against the coronavirus." [158]

After a new government was formed in May 2020, and Bennett opted for the opposition benches rather than join it, he appointed himself shadow coronavirus minister. He continued the fight against the virus even after leaving the government.

With Netanyahu failing to deal effectively with the second wave of the coronavirus and with demonstrations against the government intensifying, Bennett gained increasing support.

He had no ministry, no political status or position. Nevertheless, he took to the street and presented his own plan to handle the crisis. He ran from one TV studio to the following. He seeded social networks with his solutions, proposing initiatives, presenting strategies, and meeting with victims of the pandemic's economic fallout, standing out against the backdrop of the government's failure to stem the disease." [159]

He moved to broaden his appeal by releasing plans to contain COVID-19 and aid the economy.

Epilogue

Despite the political scene remaining as fragmented as before, in May 2020, with the world gripped by the coronavirus pandemic, Netanyahu managed to assemble a government with Benny Gantz. The two declaring they had put aside their differences. Under the terms of the deal, Netanyahu remained prime minister while a new position, alternate prime minister, was created for Gantz. It assumedly meant that after two years, he would become the next premier.

Bennett, however, stuck to his guns. He refused to join the coalition, blaming Netanyahu for not correctly engaging in negotiations with *Yamina,* the political camo he had created with Ayelet Shaked.

Though a coalition was finally forged, Netanyahu and Gantz, never at ease with each other, broke-up.

After failing to adopt a budget, the *Knesset* was dissolved on December 23 and their coalition dissolved after just over six months.

New elections, the fourth in two years, were called for March 23, 2021.

At 11:35 p.m. on June 3, 2021 calling from the sixth floor of the Kfar Maccabiah Hotel, Naftali Bennett and Yair Lapid informed then-president Reuven Rivlin that the improbable had happened.

They had succeeded in cobbling a coalition of diverse and even opposite political parties.

June 13, 2021, marked the beginning of something new in Israel.

It was the realization, at least for half of the country's political elite, that as important as having convictions in life is to have common sense.

A few months earlier, on August 5, 2020, stifling tears Bennet delivered a poignant and passionate rebuke at the *Knesset*

> *"Are you crazy? What did you do? What did you do? You are ruining the lives of millions of citizens of the State of Israel. You are killing them! Children with disabilities will not have solutions because you are fighting among yourself. What else do I have to do? What? God help us!"*
>
> *When I was defense minister, I worked on Saturdays. I desecrated Shabbat because I considered it is saving a life. It is saving a life! People are dying! What are you doing? You cannot blame anyone but yourselves.*

Dr. Michal Tsur, who was one of the partners who together with Bennett created the security company Cyota, said about him in an interview in Israel's media Calcalist at the end of 2020:

> "I don't hold the same political views as Bennett, but I do appreciate his set of values that are behind his political activity. He cares about the country and its existence and that is what led him into politics. We talk all the time and I also appreciate many of his characteristics which I don't see with other politicians, like setting a personal example or the ability to surround yourself with very talented, creative and smart people."

Eight parties: three from the right, two from the center, two from the left, and one Arab, heard Bennett and Lapid's message.

And on June 13, in the words of author Yossi Klein Halevi

> "There was the Israel of desecration, MKs shouting, faces contorted with hate, trampling on the dignity of the state as they refused to allow the prime minister-designate to speak at his own inauguration.
> And there was the Israel of Naftali Bennet and Yair Lapid, speaking with passion and reason and self-control as they presented their coalition of healing. "[160]

Twenty-seven cabinet members, two of them Arabs, one Druze and one Muslim; nine women, three Jewish law observant men with covered head. Five of them immigrants, born in Ethiopia, Morocco, and the former Soviet Union, leading what Yossi Klein Halevi accurately describes as the "Israel project."

Hard as it is to visualize it, this is the same Israel than more than two thousand years ago was driven by the same dynamic that resulted from the clashes between kings, prophets and priests.

Behind all efforts to parse the present situation with political ideas such as left and right, nationalism and cosmopolitanism, and ten of other concepts, there is the same confrontation that faced biblical prophets such as Jeremiah: knowing when to let the past go and keep on going towards the future.

Despite their fondness for the past, Jews live in the future. How could it be otherwise?

"For I know the plans I have for you, says the Lord, plans for welfare and not for evil, to give you a future and a hope" (Jeremiah 29: 11)

References

Abramov, Zalman, S.: *Perpetual Dilemma: Jewish religion in the Jewish state* (Associated University Presses, New Jersey, 1979)

Agus, Jacob, Bernard: *High priest of rebirth: the life, times, and thought of Abraham Isaac Kuk* (Bloch Publishing Company, New York, 1972)

Aran, Gideon: "Redemption as a catastrophe: the gospel of Gush Emunim," in *Religious radicalism and politics in the Middle East,* Emmanuel Sivan and Menachem Friedman (Eds.) (State University of New York Press, New York, 1990), pp. 157- 175

___ "Jewish Zionist Fundamentalism," in Martin E. Marty and R. Scott Appleby (Eds.) *Fundamentalisms Observed* (The University of Chicago Press, Chicago and London, 1994) pp. 265- 344

___ " The father, the son, and the holy land," in *Spokesmen for the despised: fundamentalist leaders of the Middle East*, R, Scott Appleby, ed. (The University of Chicago Press, Chicago, 1997), pp. 294- 327

Armstrong, Karen: *The battle for God* (Alfred A. Knopf, New York, 2000)

Aronoff, Yael, S.: *The Political Psychology of Israeli Prime Ministers When Hard-Liners Opt for Peace* (Cambridge University Press, New York, 2014)

Asa-El, Amotz: "Middle Israel: Voters shoved entire political system into the bag of cats," "The Jerusalem Post," October 4, 2019

Avishai, Bernard: *The tragedy of Zionism: how its revolutionary past haunts Israeli democracy* (Helios Press, New York, 2002)

Ben-Shlomo, Yoseph: "In defense of settlement: an interview with Professor Yoseph Ben- Shlomo," "Tikkun," Vol. 2, No2, spring 1987, pp. 72- 77

Ben Zion, Ilan: "Jewish Home MK calls for a Third Temple in Jerusalem," "The Times of Israel," 30 July 2012

Ben-Dor, Calev: "Naftali Bennett and Israel's (divided) National Religious Community: A Guide for the Perplexed," "Fathom Journal," June 2021

Bennett, Naftali: "An Hour with Naftali Bennett: Is the Right-Wing Newcomer the New Face of Israel?" "Time," Jan. 18, 2013

Bennett, Naftali: "Bennett: I'm more right-wing than Bibi, but I don't use the tools of hate," "Times of Israel," 24 February 2021

Callick, Rowan: "Thoroughly modern minister Naftali Bennett looks east for Israel's future," "The Australian.com," December 20, 2012

Carmeli, Gilad: "Cabinet minutes reveal failure to detect escalation on eve of 2014 Gaza war," "Ynet News.com", 02.28.17

Carter, Jimmy: *We can have peace in the holy land: a plan that will work*, (Simon & Schuster, New York, 2009)

Caspit, Ben: "Lapid-Bennett Alliance Shakes Up Israeli Politics," "al-Monitor," March 5, 2013

___ *The Netanyahu Years* (Thomas Dunne Books. St. Martin's Press, New York, 2017)

___"Israel's defense minister rises to the COVID-19 threat," "Al- Monitor," April 2, 2020

___ "Naftali Bennett offers new, fresh, image with lots of leadership," "Al- Monitor," November 13, 2020

___"Naftali Bennett could be Israel's next prime minister," Al- Monitor," May 7, 2021

Chafets, Zev, A match made in heaven. American Jews, Christian Zionists, and one man's exploration of the weird and wonderful judeo- evangelical alliance (Harper Perennial, New York, 2008)

___ "For Naftali Bennett, It Was Never About the Money," June 14, 2021

Erlanger, Steven and Kershner, Isabel: "Israel and Hamas Trade Attacks as Tension Rises," "The New York Times," July 8, 2014

Coren, Ora: "Naftali Bennett Has Transformed Israel's Trade Ministry, Both in Name and in Agenda," "Haaretz," May 19, 2013

Douek, Daniel: "Lawmaker backs segregated Jewish, Arab maternity wards," "The Times of Israel," April 2016

Eldar, Shlomi: "Israel's defense minister rises to the COVID-19 threat," "Al- Monitor," April 2, 2020

Estrin, Daniel: "Philosopher Micah Goodman is an Unofficial Counsel to Israel's Prime Minister," "NPR," August 25, 2021

Ettinger, Yair: "Naftali Bennett - Not What the Religious Zionists Expected," "Haaretz," Mar. 13, 2013

Evron, Boas: *Jewish State or Israeli Nation?* (Indiana University Press. Bloomington & Indianapolis, 1995)

Fisch, Harold: *The Zionist revolution: a new perspective* (St. Martin's Press, New York, 1978)

Freedman, Shalom: *Rabbi Shlomo Goren: Torah sage and general* (Urim Publications, Jerusalem, New York, 2006)

Friedman, Menachem:" The State of Israel as a theological dilemma," in *The Israeli state and society: boundaries and frontiers*, Baruch Kimmerling, ed. (State

University of New York Press, Albany, N. Y., 1989), pp 165- 215

___ " The ultra- orthodox in Israeli politics," "Jerusalem Letter," VP: 104 (Center for Public Affairs, Jerusalem, July 1990)

___ " Jewish Zealots: conservative versus innovative," in *Jewish fundamentalism in comparative perspective: religion, ideology, and the crisis of modernity*, Laurence J. Silberstein, ed. (New York University Press, New York, 1993) PP. 148-163

___ " Haredi violence in contemporary Israeli society," in *Jews and violence: images, ideologies, realities* Peter Y. Medding Eds. (Oxford University Press, New York, 2002), pp. 186- 197

Friedman, Robert I.: *Zealots for Zion: inside Israel's West Bank settlement movement* (Rutgers University Press, 1994)

Gazit, Shlomo, Trapped Fools: *Thirty Years of Israel Policy in the Territories* (Frank Cass, London, 2003)

Girard, René: *Violence and the sacred*: Trans. Patrick Gregory (The John Hopkins University Press, Baltimore, 1979)

Goldberg, Jeffrey: "The New Yorker," May 31, 2004

Goodman, Micah: *Catch-67: The Left, the Right, and the Legacy of the Six-Day War* (Dvir-Publishing House Ltd., 2017)

___ "How to Shrink the Israeli-Palestinian Conflict," "The Atlantic," January 28, 2021

___ "Eight Steps to Shrink the Israeli-Palestinian Conflict," "The Atlantic," April 1, 2019

Goren, Shlomo Elyashiv: "Problems of a religious state," in *Religious Zionism: an anthology*, Yosef Tirosh ed. (The World Zionist Organization. The Department for Torah education and Culture in the Diaspora. Organization and Information Department, Jerusalem, 1975), pp.180- 187

Gorenberg, Gershom: *The end of days: fundamentalism and the struggle for the Temple Mount* (The Free Press, New York, 2000)

___ *The accidental empire: Israel and the birth of settlements, 1967- 1977* (Times Books, New York, 2006)

___ *The unmaking of Israel*, (Harper Collins Publisher, Ltd. London/New York, 2011)

Gottesman, Evan: "Israel's Right Ascendant," "Israel Policy Forum," February 13, 2019

Greenberg, Irving, "Toward a principled pluralism, "in *Towards the twenty- first century: Judaism and the*

Jewish people in Israel and America. Essays in honor of rabbi Leon Kronish on the occasion of his seventieth birthday, Ronald Kronish, ed. (Ktav Pub, New York, 1988)

___ "The ethics of Jewish power," in *Contemporary Jewish ethics and morality*, Elliot N Dorff & Louis E. Newman, eds. (Oxford University Press, New York, Oxford, 1995) pp. 403- 421

Gur, Haviv Rettig: "Western Wall egalitarian plaza greeted with skepticism," "The Times of Israel", 25 August 2013

___ "Can the Haredi parties afford a long stay in the opposition?" "The Times of Israel," June 23, 2021

Halpern, Ben: *The idea of the Jewish state*, (Harvard University Press, Cambridge, Massachusetts, 1969)

Harel, Amos: "Tunnels, Kugel and War: Israel's Young Right-wing Minister and His Secret Army Contacts," "Haaretz," Sep. 17, 2014 Updated: Apr. 10, 2018

___ "15 Years On, Mistakes of Second Lebanon War Dictate Israel's Next Moves," "Haaretz," Jul. 16, 2021

Harel, Amos; Ettinger, Yair and Lior, Ilan: "Former IDF Chief Rabbi Suspected of Leaking Secret Gaza War Info to Bennett," "Haaretz," Sep. 16, 2014, Updated: Apr. 10, 2018

Heilman, Samuel C.: "Quiescent and active fundamentalisms: the Jewish cases," in *Accounting for fundamentalisms: the dynamic character of movements*. Martin E. Marty and R. Scott Appleby (eds.) (The University of Chicago Press, Chicago and London, 1994), pp. 173-196

___" Guides of the faithful: contemporary religious Zionist rabbis," in *Spokesmen for the despised: fundamentalist leaders of the Middle East*, R, Scott Appleby, ed. (The University of Chicago Press, Chicago, 1997), pp. 328- 362

Heilman, Samuel C. and Friedman, Menachem: "Religious Fundamentalism and Religious Jews: The Case of the Haredim," in *Fundamentalisms Observed*, Martin E. Marty, R. Scott Appleby, (eds.) (The University of Chicago Press, Chicago, 1991), pp. 197-264

Heilman, Uriel: "On Israeli religious reforms, Naftali Bennett still figuring out road map," "JTA," Nov. 19, 2013

Hermann, Tamar and Newman, David "The dove and the skullcap: secular and religious divergence in the Israeli peace camp," in *Religious and secular conflict and accommodation between Jews in Israel*, Charles S. Liebman ed. (Keter Publishing House, Jerusalem, 1990)

Horovitz, David: "Bennett: I'm more right-wing than Bibi, but I don't use the tools of hate," "Times of Israel," 24 February 2021

Hertzberg, Arthur, "Israel: the tragedy of victory," in *A Middle East reader: selected essays on the Middle East from the New York Review of Books*, Robert B. Silvers and Barbara Epstein, Eds. (The New York Review of Books, New York, 1991), pp. 58- 75

Herzog, Chaim, The Arab-Israeli wars: war and peace in the Middle East from the 1948 war of independence to the present (Vintage Book, New York, 2005)

Hovel, Revital: "Deconstructing Naftali Bennett: Growing Up to Be a Leader," "Haaretz," Jan. 18, 2013

Inbari, Motti: *Messianic Religious Zionism Confronts Israeli Territorial Compromises* (Cambridge University Press, New York, 2012)

Isaac, Rael Jean, *Israel divided: ideological politics in the Jewish state* (The Johns Hopkins University Press, Baltimore and London, 1976)

Jeffay, Nathan: "Losing a Mentor, Gaining an Opponent," "Forward," August 25, 2010

Karpin, Michael and Friedman, Ina: *Murder in the name of God the plot to kill Yitzhak Rabin* (Henry Holt, New York, 1998)

Katz, Jacob, Exclusiveness and tolerance: studies in Jewish- Gentile relations in Medieval and Modern times, (Behrman House, Inc. NJ, 1961)

___ "Israel and the Messiah," in *Essential papers on messianic movements and personalities in Jewish history*, Marc Saperstein (ed.) (New York University Press, New York and London, 1992) pp. 475- 491.

Kessler, Oren: "The Meaning of Israel's First Religious Prime Minister," "Foreign Policy," June 7, 2021

Kimball, Charles: *When religion becomes evil* (Harper Collins, San Francisco, 2003)

Kimmerling, Baruch: *The invention and decline of Israeliness: state, society, and the military* (University of California Press, Berkeley, Los Angeles, London, 2001)

King, Laura: "He 'won the lottery' of Israeli politics. But Naftali Bennett remains an enigma," Los Angeles Times," June 10, 2021

Kingsley, Patrick: "Israel Moves Toward Coalition Deal That Could Sideline Netanyahu," "The New York Times," May 30, 2021

Knohl, Dov: *Siege in the hills of Hebron: the battle of the Etzion Bloc* (Kfar Etzion Educational Center, Boys Town Jerusalem, 1989)

Kook, Zvi Yehuda "Zionism and biblical prophecy," in *Religious Zionism: an anthology*, Yosef Tirosh ed. (The World Zionist Organization. The Department for Torah Education and Culture in the Diaspora. Organization and Information Department, Jerusalem, 1975)

Laqueur, Walter: *A history of Zionism* (Schoken Books, New York, 1972)

Lehmann, David and Siebzehner, Batia, *Remaking Israeli Judaism the challenge of Shas* (Hurst Company, London, 2006)

Leibowitz, Yeshayahu: *Judaism, human values, and the Jewish state* (Harvard University Press, Cambridge, Massachusetts, 1995)

Levinson, Chaim: "Bennett Moves Habayit Hayehudi Ticket Slightly to the Left," "Haaretz," Jan. 28, 2015

___ "Soccer Star Eli Ohana Quits Habayit Hayehudi, Amid Criticism," "Haaretz," Jan. 29, 2015

Littman, Shany: "Deconstructing Naftali Bennett: The Start-up Years," "Haaretz," January 18, 2013

Lubell, Maayan: "For Habayit Hayehudi, an independent Palestine amounts to 'suicide' for Israel," Haaretz," Feb. 26, 2015

Lustick, S. Ian: *For the land and the Lord: Jewish fundamentalism in Israel* (Council of Foreign Relations, New York, 1988)

___ " Jewish fundamentalism and the Israeli-Palestinian impasse," in *Jewish fundamentalism in comparative perspective: religion, ideology, and the crisis of modernity* Laurence J. Silberstein ed. (New York University, New York, 1993)

Magid, Jacob: "How did 2 of Israel's most prominent ministers end up outside the 21st Knesset?" "The Times of Israel," 12 April 2019

Mamlak, Gershon: "On the Integrity of Judaism," in *Essays on the Thought and Philosophy of Rabbi Kook*, Ezra Gellman (ed.) (Cornwall Books, New York, London, Toronto, 1991)

Margalit, Ruth: "How the Religious Right Transformed Israeli Education," "The New Yorker," August 23, 2019

Mergui, Raphael: *Israel's ayatollahs: Meir Kahane and the far right in Israel*, (Saqi Books, London, 1987)

Meyer, Michal: "A city won by accident," *Jerusalem Post*, May 31, 2002

Miller, Emanuel: "Who Is Israel's New Prime Minister Naftali Bennett?" "Honest Report," June 16, 2021

Morgenstern, Arie: *Hastening redemption: messianism and the resettlement of the land of Israel*. Joel A. Linsider, trans. (Oxford University Press, Oxford, 2006)

Morris, Benny: *The road to Jerusalem: Glubb Pasha, Palestine and the Jews* (I.B. Tauris, London, 2003)

Mualem, Mazal: "Netanyahu's New Strongman," "Al-Monitor," March 15, 2013

___ "Netanyahu bitter over justice minister appointee," "Israel Pulse," May 8, 2015

___ "Netanyahu critic wins prestigious literary award," "Al-Monitor, June 16, 2017

___ "The 'Bennett and Shaked' brand: Israel's political stars fall to earth," "Al-Monitor," April 17, 2019

___ "Could Bloc for Change really replace Netanyahu?" "Al-Monitor," April 27, 2021

Much, Afif Abu: "In first for Israel, Arab party speaks with official voice in coalition talks," "Al-Monitor," June 2, 2021

Oren, B. Michael: *Six days of War: June 1967 and the Making of the Modern Middle East*, (Random House Publishing Group, United States of America, 2002, 2003)

Pfeffer, Anshel: Bibi: *The Turbulent Life and Times of Benjamin Netanyahu,* (Basic Books, New York, 2018)

Pfeffer, Anshel: "Naftali Bennett, Next Israeli PM: The Man Behind the Slogans and Stereotypes," "Haaretz," Jun. 13, 2021

Rael, Isaac, Jean: *Israel divided: ideological politics in the Jewish state* (The Johns Hopkins University Press, Baltimore and London, 1976)

Ravid, Barak: "Deconstructing Naftali Bennett: The Netanyahu Years," "Haaretz," Jan. 18, 2013, Updated: Apr. 10, 2018

Ravitzky, Aviezer, "Roots of Kahanism: consciousness and political reality," *The Jerusalem Quarterly*, No. 39, 1986, pp. 90- 108

___" Religious radicalism and political messianism," in *Religious Radicalism and Politics in the Middle East*. Emmanuel Sivan and Menachem Friedman, Eds. (State University of New York Press, New York, 1990)

___*Messianism, Zionism, and Jewish religious radicalism*, trans. Michael Swirsky and Jonathan Chipman (University of Chicago Press, Chicago, 1993).

___" Let us search our path": religious Zionism after the Assassination," in *The assassination of Yitzhak Rabin*, Yoram Peri ed. (Stanford University Press, Stanford, California, 2000), pp. 141- 162

Remnick, David: "The Party Faithful," "The New Yorker," January 21, 2013

Rosenberg, Yai: "Why Naftali Bennett Decapitated the Settler Right and What It Means for Israel's Future," "Tablet Magazine," January 15, 2019

Rosner, Shmuel and Fuchs, Camil: *Israeli Judaism: Portrait of a Cultural Revolution* (The Jewish People Institute, Jerusalem, 2019)

Ross, Dennis: *The missing peace: the inside story of the fight for Middle East peace* (Farrar, Straus and Giroux, New York, 2004)

Roth-Avneir, Danielle: "A New Chapter in Israeli Politics," "Algemeiner," June 15, 2021

Rudoren, Jodi: "Dynamic Former Netanyahu Aide Shifts Israeli Campaign Rightward," "The New York Times," Dec. 26, 2012

Sachar, Howard, M.: *A History of Israel: From the rise of Zionism to our time*, (Alfred A. Knoppf, New York, 2007)

Schwartz, Dov: *Faith at the crossroads: a theological profile of religious Zionism*. Trans. Batya Stein (Brill, Boston, 2002)

Schweid, Eliezer: *The land of Israel: national home or land of destiny*. Trans. Deborah Greniman (Associated University Presses, London and Toronto, 1985)

Segal, Haggai: *Dear brothers: The West Bank Jewish Underground* (Beit- Shammai Publication, Woodmere N. Y., 1988)

Shaked, Ayelet: "An Interview with Ayelet Shaked," August 15, 2012. http://yoelmeltzer.com/an-interview-with-ayelet-

Shapira, Anita: *Israel: A History* (Brandeis University Press, Waltham, Massachusetts, 2012)

Sharon, Jeremy: "Bayit Yehudi is over - Does their public need a party anymore?" "The Jerusalem Post," February 7, 2021

Shavit, Ari (*Haaretz, Friday Magazine*, March 22, 2002) in Amon, Moshe: "Terrorism and Political Violence," Vol. 16, Spring 2004, Number 1, pp.53-54

Sherwood, Harriet: "Interview Naftali Bennett interview: 'There won't be a Palestinian state within Israel'" "The Guardian," Mon 7 Jan 2013

Sprinzak, Ehud: "Unrestrained intercommunal violence; the case of Rabbi Kahane and Kach," in *Fundamentalisms and the state: remaking polities, economies and militance* Martin E. Marty; F. Scott Appleby; R. Scott Appleby (Eds.) (University of Chicago Press, Chicago, 1996), pp. 477- 490

___*Brother against brother: violence and extremism in Israeli Politics from Altalena to the Rabin Assassination* (Free Press, New York, 1999)

___"Rational fanatics," *Foreign Policy* September/October 2000

___" Israel's radical right and the countdown to the Rabin assassination," in *The assassination of Yitzhak Rabin*, Yoram Peri ed. (Stanford University Press, Stanford, California, 2000), pp. 96-128

Srivastava, Mehull: "Naftali Bennett reaps reward for calculated rise to summit of Israeli politics," "Financial Times," June 9, 2021

Stub, Zev: "Israel Elections: Which economic plan does Israel really need?" "The Jerusalem Post," March 17, 2021

Taub, Gadi: *The Settlers: And the struggle over the meaning of Zionism*, (Yale University, 2010)

Tucker, Nati: "Executive with Ties to Netanyahu Is to Join Army Radio Supervisory Body," "Haaretz," Jun. 10, 2013

Vick, Karl: "An Hour with Naftali Bennett: Is the Right-Wing Newcomer the New Face of Israel?" "Time," Jan. 18, 2013

Vidal, Elihay: "Israel PM Bennett nets millions from Payoneer SPAC offering," 24.06.21, https://www.calcalistech.com/ctech/articles/0,7340,L-3909653,00.html

Vital, David, *Zionism: the formative years* (Clarendon Press, Oxford, 2001)

Wiener, Julie: "Who is Ayelet Shaked, Israel's new justice minister?" "The Times of Israel," Friday, May 8, 2015

Winer, Stuart: "Jewish Home approves major party changes," "The Times of Israel," 11 September 2014

Wootliff, Raoul: "Bennett, Shaked quit Jewish Home, announce formation of 'The New Right'," "The Times of Israel," December 2018

___ "Yamina party officially splits into New Right, Jewish Home-National Union," "The Times of Israel," 10 October 2019

___ "Yamina No. 3 Alon Davidi quits incoming Knesset before being sworn in," "Times of Israel," 5 April 2021

___ "Bennett: 'I told my kids their father will be the most hated person in Israel' "The Times of Israel," 4 June 2021

Yudelson, Larry: "When Israel's prime minister lived in Teaneck," "Jewish Standard," June 16, 2021

Zertal, Idith and Eldar, Akiva: *The Lords of the Land: The War Over Israel's Settlements in the Occupied Territories, 1967- 2007.* (Nation Books, New York, 2007)

Zilber, Neri: "The Tent Protest: Israel's Social-Democratic Movement," "Dissent," August 3, 2011

Ziv, Guy: Can Bennet, a Right-Wing Provocateur, Save Israel's Democracy," "Haaretz," June 13, 2021

Footnotes/ Endnotes

[1] Baron, S. W.: *A Social and Religious History of the Jews*, Vol. I. p. 26

[2] Greenberg, Irving: "The Ethics of Jewish Power," in *Contemporary Jewish Ethics and Morality: A reader*, Elliot N. Dorff & Louis E. Newman (eds.), p. 420

[3] (1762-1839)

[4] ("ultra- orthodox Jews")

[5] Hartman, Donniel: *The Boundaries of Judaism*, p. 111

[6] Moses Sofer [Hatam Sofer], "Eleh Divrei Habrit" [These are the words of the Covenant] (originally published in 1819, in *The Jew in the Modern World*, ed. Mendes- Flohr and Yehuda Reinharz (New York: Oxford University Press, 1980), pp. 32 ff.

[7] Moses Sofer, *Responsa Hatam Sofer, O. H.* 28, 148, and 181; *Y.D.* 19 and 286

[8] (1865-1935)

[9] Agus, J. B.: *Guideposts in Modern Judaism*, p.36

[10] Aran, Gideon: "The Father, the Son, and the Holy Land," in *Spokesmen For The Despised: Fundamentalist Leaders of the Middle East*, R. Scott Appleby, ed., p. 300

[11] "In Hebrew, there's no word, no accurate translation, for "competence." We need a word for it, and we certainly need competence." Bennett, Naftali: "Bennett: I'm more right-wing than Bibi, but I don't use the tools of hate," "Times of Israel," 24 February 2021

[12] Rosner, Shmuel and Fuchs, Camil: *Israelite Judaism: Portrait of a Cultural Revolution* (Kindle loc. 134)

[13] *Ibid.* (Kindle loc. 102)

[14] Gur, Haviv Rettig: "Can the Haredi parties afford a long stay in the opposition?" "The Times of Israel," June 23, 2021

[15] The Israeli Parliament

[16] Littman, Shany: "Deconstructing Naftali Bennett: The Start-up Years," "Haaretz," January 18, 2013
[17] *Ibid.*
[18] *Ibid.*
[19] *Ibid.*
[20] Remnick, David: "The Party Faithful," "The New Yorker," January 21, 2013
[21] Israel Defense Forces
[22] "General Staff Reconnaissance Unit"
[23] Yudelson, Larry: "When Israel's prime minister lived in Teaneck," "Jewish Standard," June 16, 2021
[24] That this feeling finds an agreement of sorts in much of the Israeli population has been expressed by Israeli journalist Amos Harel in a July 16, 2021 article in the newspaper "Haaretz," "Every conversation with officers who fought then as company and battalion commanders and have since been promoted triggers two analyses. First, they believe the army functioned even more chaotically in that war than previously believed.
Second, the preparations before a possible war in Lebanon or Gaza in the future are based on correcting the mistakes of 2006. The lessons stand out in a number of areas: polishing the operative plans, streamlining the production and use of intelligence, and improving the work of the command posts." (Harel, Amos; "15 Years On, Mistakes of Second Lebanon War Dictate Israel's Next Moves," "Haaretz," Jul. 16, 2021)
[25] Bennett, Naftali quoted by Kessler, Oren: "The Meaning of Israel's First Religious Prime Minister," "Foreign Policy," June 7, 2021
[26] He was defeated in the 1999 elections by Ehud Barak
[27] Under his leadership the party had succeeded to win no more than twelve Knesset seats while Ehud Olmert from the centrist Kadima party had become Israel's 12th prime minister
[28] Shaked, Ayelet: "An Interview with Ayelet Shaked," August 15, 2012. http://yoelmeltzer.com/an-interview-with-ayelet-
[29] Caspit, Ben: *The Netanyahu Years* (Kindle Loc. 3258)

[30] Hovel, Revital: "Deconstructing Naftali Bennett: Growing Up to Be a Leader," "Haaretz," Jan. 18, 2013

[31] Ravid, Barak: "Deconstructing Naftali Bennett: The Netanyahu Years," "Haaretz," Jan. 18, 2013, Updated: Apr. 10, 2018

[32] Caspit, Ben: *The Netanyahu Years* (Kindle Loc. 3269)

[33] Mualem, Mazal: "Netanyahu bitter over justice minister appointee," "Israel Pulse," May 8, 2015

[34] Tucker, Nati: "Executive with Ties to Netanyahu Is to Join Army Radio Supervisory Body," "Haaretz," Jun. 10, 2013

[35] Ravid, Barak: "Deconstructing Naftali Bennett: The Netanyahu Years," "Haaretz," Jan. 18, 2013, Updated: Apr. 10, 2018

[36] Pfeffer, Anshel: Bibi: The Turbulent Life and Times of Benjamin Netanyahu, (Kindle loc. 5850)

[37] Littman, Shany: "Deconstructing Naftali Bennett: The Start-up Years," "Haaretz," Jan. 18, 2013

[38] *Ibid.*

[39] *Ibid.*

[40] *Ibid.*

[41] Oren, B. Michael: Six days of War: June 1967 and the Making of the Modern Middle East, p. 187

[42] Isaac, Jean Rael: Israel Divided: Ideological Politics in the Jewish State, p. 5

[43] Ben-Shlomo, Yosef: "In Defense of Settlement: An Interview with Professor Yoseph Ben-Shlomo," "Tikkun," Vol. 2, NO. 2, Spring 1987, p. 74

[44] Bar-On, Mordechai: *In Pursuit of Peace: A History of the Israeli Peace Movement*, p. 26

[45] Rabin, Yitzhak: *The Rabin Memoirs*, p. 104

[46] Sachar, M. Howard: *A History of Israel. From the Rise of Zionism to Our Time*, p. 644-645

[47] Oren, B. Michael: Six days of War: June 1967 and the Making of the Modern Middle East, p. 312

[48] In his memoirs, *My "War" with Israel*, King Hussein admitted that "we were misinformed about what happened in Egypt when the

Israelis attacked the UAR bases... These reports- fantastic to say the least- had much to do with our confusion and false interpretation of the situation."

[49] Israeli Prime Minister Levi Eshkol had sent a message to King Hussein of Jordan through General Odd Bull, the UN commander, stating that Israel would not initiate hostilities along the eastern front. The message ended: "Israel will not, repeat not, attack Jordan if Jordan maintains the quiet. But if Jordan opens hostilities, Israel will respond with all its might."

[50] Meyer, Michal: "A City won by accident," *Jerusalem Post*, May 31, 2002, p. 4

[51] Megillah 17b

[52] Shapira, Anita: *Israel: A History* (Kindle loc. 6768)

[53] Fisch, Harold: *The Zionist Revolution: A New Perspective*, p. 91

[54] Sachar, M. Howard: *A History of Israel: From the Rise of Zionism to Our Time*, p. 787

[55] http://myesha.org.il/

[56] Jeffay, Nathan: "Losing a Mentor, Gaining an Opponent," "Forward," August 25, 2010

[57] *Ibid.*

[58] Zilber, Neri: "The Tent Protest: Israel's Social-Democratic Movement," "Dissent," August 3, 2011

[59] Jeffay, Nathan; "Losing a Mentor, Gaining an Opponent," "Forward," August 25, 2010

[60] *Ibid.*

[61] Srivastava, Mehull: "Naftali Bennett reaps reward for calculated rise to summit of Israeli politics," "Financial Times," June 9, 2021

[62] Israeli philosopher and co-author of the Israeli Army Code of Ethics Moshe Halbertal. Quoted by David Reminick: "The Party Faithful," "The New Yorker," January 21, 2013

[63] *Mafdal*: acronym for *Miflagah Datit-Le'ummit* (National Religious Party)

[64] Acronym of *Mifleget Poley Eretz Israel* (Workers Party of the Land of Israel)

[65] except for a brief period in 1974
[66] The religious party would then, join all subsequent Llikud governments, except for that formed by Yitzhak Rabin in 1992.
[67] Shavit, Ari (*Haaretz, Friday Magazine*, March 22, 2002) in Amon, Moshe: "Terrorism and Political Violence," Vol. 16, Spring 2004, Number 1, pp.53-54
[68] Goldberg, Jeffrey: "The New Yorker," May 31, 2004, pp. 58- 59
[69] A forum of all the party members with voting rights
[70] It was decided that the *Mafdal* would resign from the government if:
The government approved the dismantling of Israeli settlements.
The Knesset passed laws of evacuation and compensation.
The Labor Party joined the government and the coalition.
A general referendum on the disengagement would not be held.
On 9 November 2004, after Ariel Sharon declined the *Mafdal*'s demand to hold a national referendum regarding the disengagement, Zevulun Orlev and the party resigned from the coalition and the government, vowing to pursue general elections in an effort to replace Sharon with a right-wing prime minister. After their resignation, Sharon had a minority coalition of 56 Knesset members out of 120.
[71] Ben Zion, Ilan: "Jewish Home MK calls for a Third Temple in Jerusalem," "The Times of Israel," 30 July 2012
[72] Orlev, who once had expressed his intentions of becoming prime minister, after losing the primaries announced his resignation from politics.
[73] Callick, Rowan: "Thoroughly modern minister Naftali Bennett looks east for Israel's future," "The Australian.com," December 20, 2012
[74] Asa-El, Amotz: "Middle Israel: Voters shoved entire political system into the bag of cats," "The Jerusalem Post," October 4, 2019
[75] Ettinger, Yair: "Naftali Bennett - Not What the Religious Zionists Expected," "Haaretz," Mar. 13, 2013
[76] An upper-middle class city north of Tel Aviv, in Israel proper.

[77] Bennett, Naftali: "An Hour with Naftali Bennett: Is the Right-Wing Newcomer the New Face of Israel?" "Time," Jan. 18, 2013
[78] Ibid.
[79] Wiener, Julie: "Who is Ayelet Shaked, Israel's new justice minister?" "The Times of Israel," Friday, May 8, 2015
[80] 1865-1935
[81] Agus, J. B.: *Guideposts in Modern Judaism*, p.36
[82] "The Economist," January 5th, 2013, p. 36
[83] Mualem, Mazal: "Netanyahu's New Strongman," "Al-Monitor," March 15, 2013
[84] "The Movement"
[85] "There Is a Future"
[86] on August 28, 2012
[87] Bennett, Naftali: "Bennett: I'm more right-wing than Bibi, but I don't use the tools of hate," "Times of Israel," 24 February 2021
[88] Caspit, Ben: "Lapid-Bennett Alliance Shakes Up Israeli Politics," "al-Monitor," March 5, 2013
[89] Bennett, Naftali: "Bennett: I'm more right-wing than Bibi, but I don't use the tools of hate," "Times of Israel," 24 February 2021
[90] Vick, Karl: "An Hour with Naftali Bennett: Is the Right-Wing Newcomer the New Face of Israel?" "Time," Jan. 18, 2013
[91] the ultra-orthodox, who do not serve in the army and rely heavily on welfare
[92] Bennett, Naftali: "An Hour with Naftali Bennett: Is the Right-Wing Newcomer the New Face of Israel?" "Time," Jan. 18, 2013
[93] Miller, Emanuel: "Who Is Israel's New Prime Minister Naftali Bennett?" "Honest Report," June 16, 2021
[94] Gur, Haviv Rettig: "Western Wall egalitarian plaza greeted with skepticism," "The Times of Israel", 25 August 2013
[95] Heilman, Uriel: "On Israeli religious reforms, Naftali Bennett still figuring out road map," "JTA," Nov. 19, 2013
[96] Gur, Haviv Rettig: "Western Wall egalitarian plaza greeted with skepticism," "The Times of Israel", 25 August 2013
[97] On August 20, 2014

[98] The man believed to be the ringleader of the kidnapping, Hussam Qawasme, was taken in Israeli custody and convicted. Two others believed to be his accomplices remained at large. The murders led to a revenge attack during which three rightwing Israelis kidnapped and murdered 17-year-old Mohammed Abu Khdeir.

[99] Erlanger, Steven and Kershner, Isabel: "Israel and Hamas Trade Attacks as Tension Rises," "The New York Times," July 8, 2014

[100] Harel, Amos; Ettinger, Yair and Lior, Ilan: "Former IDF Chief Rabbi Suspected of Leaking Secret Gaza War Info to Bennett," "Haaretz," Sep. 16, 2014, Updated: Apr. 10, 2018

[101] *Ibid.*

[102] *Ibid.*

[103] Carmeli, Gilad: "Cabinet minutes reveal failure to detect escalation on eve of 2014 Gaza war," "Ynet News.com", 02.28.17

[104] Bennett, Naftali: "An Hour with Naftali Bennett: Is the Right-Wing Newcomer the New Face of Israel?" "Time," Jan. 18, 2013

[105] *Ibid.*

[106] "Bennett, Lapid offer conflicting views on peace," "Jerusalem Post," June 21, 2013

[107] *Ibid.*

[108] "Catch- 67: The Left, the Right, and the Legacy of the Six-Day War, did not deal with the Israeli-Palestinian conflict, only the broken Israeli discussion about the conflict." Goodman, Micah: "Eight Steps to Shrink the Israeli-Palestinian Conflict," "The Atlantic," April 1, 2019

[109] Goodman, Micah: "How to Shrink the Israeli-Palestinian Conflict," "The Atlantic," January 28, 2021

[110] Goodman, Micah: "Eight Steps to Shrink the Israeli-Palestinian Conflict," "The Atlantic," April 1, 2019

[111] Pfeffer, Anshel: "Naftali Bennett, Next Israeli PM: The Man Behind the Slogans and Stereotypes," "Haaretz," Jun. 13, 2021

[112] Bennett, Naftali: 2017 Fathom Interview with Naftali Bennett," Winter of 2017

[113] Bennett, Naftali: "For Israel, Two-State Is No Solution," "The New York Times," Nov. 5, 2014
[114] *Ibid.*
[115] Kessler, Oren: "The Meaning of Israel's First Religious Prime Minister," "Foreign Policy," June 7, 2021
[116] Srivastava, Mehull: "Naftali Bennett reaps reward for calculated rise to summit of Israeli politics," "Financial Times," June 9, 2021
[117] Ziv, Guy: "Can Bennett, a Right-wing Provocateur, Save Israel's Democracy?" "Haaretz," Jun. 13, 2021.
[118] Douek, Daniel: "Lawmaker backs segregated Jewish, Arab maternity wards," "The Times of Israel," April 2016
[119] *Ibid.*
[120] "In scathing statement, Bennett rejects union with Otzma Yehudit," "The Times of Israel," 15 January 2020
[121] Jeffay, Nathan: "Losing a Mentor, Gaining an Opponent," "Forward," August 25, 2010
[122] Bennett, Naftali: "For Israel, Two-State Is No Solution," "The New York Times," Nov. 5, 2014
[123] Bennett, Naftali: 2017 Fathom Interview with Naftali Bennett," Winter of 2017
[124] Lubell, Maayan: "For Habayit Hayehudi, an independent Palestine amounts to 'suicide' for Israel," Haaretz," Feb. 26, 2015
[125] Bennett, Naftali: 2017 Fathom Interview with Naftali Bennett," Winter of 2017
[126] Bennett, Naftali: "Bennett: I'm more right-wing than Bibi, but I don't use the tools of hate," "Times of Israel," 24 February 2021
[127] Coren, Ora: "Naftali Bennett Has Transformed Israel's Trade Ministry, Both in Name and in Agenda," "Haaretz," May 19, 2013
[128] Sherwood, Harriet: "Interview Naftali Bennett interview: 'There won't be a Palestinian state within Israel'" "The Guardian," Mon 7 Jan 2013

[129] Callick, Rowan: "Thoroughly modern minister Naftali Bennett looks east for Israel's future," "The Australian.com," December 20, 2012
[130] Bennett, Naftali: "Putting All Israelis to Work," "The New York Times," Feb. 13, 2014
[131] Bennett, Naftali: "An Hour with Naftali Bennett: Is the Right-Wing Newcomer the New Face of Israel?" "Time," Jan. 18, 2013
[132] "What is Bennett's 'Singapore Plan' for the Israeli economy?" "Allisrael.com," March 14, 2021
[133] Bennett, Naftali: "Bennett: I'm more right-wing than Bibi, but I don't use the tools of hate," "Times of Israel," 24 February 2021
[134] Prime Minister Benjamin Netanyahu, Jerusalem, December 2, 2014
[135] What the tradition call *K'lal Yisrael*.
[136] "[…] Kook's conviction that Divine providence was at work in the changes being brought about by secularists; above all, the Jewish rebirth in the land of Israel." Sacks, Jonathan: One People? Tradition, Modernity and Jewish Unity, p. 182
[137] Winer, Stuart: "Jewish Home approves major party changes," "The Times of Israel," 11 September 2014
[138] Levinson, Chaim: "Bennett Moves Habayit Hayehudi Ticket Slightly to the Left," "Haaretz," Jan. 28, 2015
[139] Levinson, Chaim: "Soccer Star Eli Ohana Quits Habayit Hayehudi, Amid Criticism," "Haaretz," Jan. 29, 2015
[140] Asa-El, Amotz: "His first great misstep: The humbling of Naftali Bennett," "The Jerusalem Post," January 31, 2015
[141] Rosenberg, Yai: "Why Naftali Bennett Decapitated the Settler Right and What It Means for Israel's Future," "Tablet Magazine," January 15, 2019
[142] Mualem, Mazal: "The 'Bennett and Shaked' brand: Israel's political stars fall to earth," "Al-Monitor," April 17, 2019
[143] Margalit, Ruth: "How the Religious Right Transformed Israeli Education," "The New Yorker" August 23, 2019

[144] Miller, Emanuel: "Who Is Israel's New Prime Minister Naftali Bennett?" "Honest Report," June 16, 2021
[145] *Ibid.*
[146] Henri Lévy Bernard: "Pondering, Discussing, Traveling Amid and Defending the Inevitable War," August 6, 2006
[147] Mualem, Mazal, "Netanyahu critic wins prestigious literary award," "Al-Monitor, June 16, 2017
[148] Goldberg, Jeffrey: "The Atlantic," May 2008, pp. 42- 43
[149] Sharon, Jeremy: Chief Rabbi Yosef: Science, math are nonsense, study in yeshiva instead," "The Jerusalem Post," June 30, 2021
[150] Wootliff, Raoul: "Bennett, Shaked quit Jewish Home, announce formation of 'The New Right'," "The Times of Israel," December 2018,
[151] Gottesman, Evan: "Israel's Right Ascendant," "Israel Policy Forum," February 13, 2019
[152] Magid, Jacob: "How did 2 of Israel's most prominent ministers end up outside the 21st Knesset?" "The Times of Israel," 12 April 2019
[153] "Leaked recordings reveal Sara Netanyahu's efforts to sabotage URWP-Shaked merger," "Times of Israel," July 2019
[154] Miller, Emanuel: "Who Is Israel's New Prime Minister Naftali Bennett?" "Honest Report," June 16, 2021
[155] Eldar, Shlomi: "Israel's defense minister rises to the COVID-19 threat," "Al- Monitor," April 2, 2020
[156] *Ibid.*
[157] *Ibid*
[158] *Ibid.*
[159] Caspit, Ben: "Is Israel ready for a religious prime minister?" "Al Monitor," August 11, 2020
[160] Klein Halevi, Yossi: "Why this fractious coalition gives me hope," "The Times of Israel," June 14, 2021

www.ingramcontent.com/pod-product-compliance
Lightning Source LLC
Chambersburg PA
CBHW072007290426
44109CB00018B/2162